Study Guide for

BROADCASTING IN AMERICA

Study Guide for

BROADCASTING IN AMERICA

A Survey of Electronic Media

FIFTH EDITION

Sydney W. Head
University of Miami

Christopher H. Sterling
The George Washington University

with contributions by

Susan Tyler Eastman, *Indiana University*
Lemuel B. Schofield, *University of Miami*

Norman Felsenthal
Temple University

Houghton Mifflin Company
Boston
Dallas Geneva, Ill. Lawrenceville, N.J. Palo Alto

Printed in the U.S.A.

Library of Congress Catalog Card Number: 86-81342

ISBN: 0-395-38779-5

BCDEFGHIJ-B-8987

Contents

Preface		vii
PROLOGUE	**The World of Broadcasting**	1
Chapter 1	Global Context	3
PART 1	**Development**	11
Chapter 2	The Rise of Radio	13
3	From Radio to Television	23
4	Era of Electronic Media	31
PART 2	**Technology**	39
Chapter 5	Basic Physical Concepts	41
6	Technology of Traditional Broadcasting	49
7	Delivery, Distribution, and Storage	59
PART 3	**Economics**	69
Chapter 8	Stations, Systems, and Networks	71
9	Broadcast and Cable Advertising	79
10	Other Economic Aspects of Electronic Media	91
PART 4	**Programming**	101
Chapter 11	Programming Problems, Processes, and Practices	103
12	Network Programs	111
13	Nonnetwork Programs	121

PART 5	**Effects**	129
Chapter 14	Audience Measurement and Testing	131
15	Social Consequences	141
PART 6	**Controls**	151
Chapter 16	Agencies of Control	153
17	FCC Administration of the Law	163
18	Freedom and Fairness	177
EPILOGUE	**Future of Electronic Media**	189
Chapter 19	Future Prospects	191
Answer Key		195

Preface

This *Study Guide* is designed to help students process and review the material contained in the fifth edition of *Broadcasting in America.* I have worked closely with the authors of the text to insure that this guide complements their material. Each chapter of the *Study Guide* covers the parallel chapter in the text and is organized as follows:

1. *Chapter Focus:* This short section contains one to three paragraphs and is designed to give you an overview of the chapter.
2. *Capsule:* The most significant points from each section of every chapter are summarized here. The intent is to synthesize important facts and issues and present them in a way that will help you recall the more detailed discussion contained in the text.
3. *Key Terms:* This series of sentences, each containing one or more blanks, has been created to help you recall and understand the extensive terminology that is related to broadcasting and other electronic media. Sentences that describe similar terms are grouped into clusters. For the most part, the terms are presented in the same order they are used in the text. Work through each key terms exercise. Then check your responses with the correct answers which are printed at the back of this *Study Guide.*
4. *Self-Test:* These items are designed to help you appraise your understanding of the material. The first series of questions are fill-ins; the remaining questions are true/false. Analyze your response to each true/false question. Which elements in the question make it true or false? How might each question be written for the opposite response to be correct? Answers to all self-test items are printed in the back of this *Study Guide.*
5. *Project:* One or more activities are suggested for each chapter. Most of these activities involve library research and suggest references where you can find additional information.

You are urged to use this book in the way that is most helpful to you. One method is to read each chapter in the text and then proceed to the corresponding chapter in the *Study Guide.* Another method is to use portions of the *Study Guide* to help you preview the material you are going to read in the text. Begin with the Chapter Focus. Then read the Capsule for each section prior to reading each section in the text. After you have completed the text, re-read the Capsule. Then proceed to the Key Terms, Self-Test, and Project.

I wish to express my appreciation to the authors of the text, especially to Chris Sterling who reviewed all of the material in this guide and made many valuable suggestions.

Norman Felsenthal
Temple University
Philadelphia, PA

Study Guide for

BROADCASTING IN AMERICA

PROLOGUE

The World of Broadcasting

CHAPTER 1

Global Context

CHAPTER FOCUS

This chapter presents material that will give you some background for your study of broadcasting as it exists in the United States as well as broadcasting as it exists in other countries of the world. Many of the concepts introduced here will be discussed more thoroughly in later chapters of the text. The American system of broadcasting is unique. Most countries regulate, program, and finance their broadcasting systems very differently. As you gain an understanding of these systems, you will be better able to assess the strengths and the weaknesses of broadcasting in America.

CAPSULE

Main points from each section of Chapter 1 are summarized below.

1.1 Convergence

A. Satellite utilization and other technological developments have added many new services to traditional telephone and broadcasting services.

B. Technical standards for television, however, differ from country to country. International exchange of TV programs requires converters.

1.2 Common Grounds

A. Broadcasters use various portions of the electromagnetic frequency spectrum. Regulation is necessary to prevent interference.

B. All governments consider the electromagnetic spectrum to be a public resource that cannot be privately owned.

1.3 Political Philosophies

A. Differing political philosophies produce differing systems of control.

B. Broadcasting in America is *permissive*, operated by private entrepreneurs, and financially supported by advertising. Permissive systems cater to commercial motivations that emphasize what people want rather than what they may need.

C. Other countries take a *paternalistic* orientation that tries to maintain a balance between wants and needs in program content.

D. Communist and Third World countries take an *authoritarian* orientation because they consider broadcasting to be an extension of the ruling government.

1.4 Pluralistic Trend

A. Neither permissivism, paternalism, nor authoritarianism exist in pure form. *Pluralism* exists when more than one motive is involved in the production, selection, and scheduling of programs.

B. U.S. broadcasting that has both commercial and noncommercial (public) elements is pluralistic, but the balance is heavily in favor of the commercial portion.

C. British broadcasting has a more equal balance between the commercial (IBA) and noncommercial (BBC) elements. British broadcasting is generally regarded as a good example of successful pluralism (Exhibit 1.1).

1.5 Legal Foundations

A. Most nations belong to the International Telecommunication Union and agree to treaties that allocate specific frequencies for specific services.

B. Broadcasting in America is classified as interstate commerce. It enjoys constitutional protection under the First Amendment as well as an elaborate regulatory scheme that results in a great deal of protection for incumbent broadcasters from arbitrary government action.

1.6 Access to the Air

A. U.S. law obligates broadcasters to grant equal opportunities for air time to all candidates for the same political office.

B. Other countries generally allocate air time to political parties rather than to individual candidates and tend to favor the party then in power.

C. Many countries are beginning to question and reduce barriers that deny individuals or groups access to broadcasting.

1.7 Economics

A. Most broadcasting systems depend on government funding (Exhibit 1.2).

B. Many European systems and NHK, the Japanese noncommercial system, depend on receiver license fees.

C. Most American broadcasters and some European systems derive their financial support from advertising. Public broadcasting in the United States derives much of its support from underwriting.

D. Pirate stations and certain transborder broadcasters (Radio-Tele-Luxembourg) transmit advertiser-supported programming to audiences.

1.8 Geography

A. It is easier to broadcast to a unified landmass such as the United States than to an archipelago of islands such as Japan or Indonesia.

B. Neighboring countries may have problems with spillover programs and transborder interference.

1.9 Programs and Schedules

A. Program content reflects the orientation and interests of the country supplying the programming.

B. International news agencies such as Associated Press, United Press International, and Reuters dominate worldwide news flow. These agencies reflect Western news values.

C. U.S. dominance in the international syndication market has led to charges of cultural imperialism.

1.10 Transborder Broadcasting

A. Many countries have external broadcasting services that transmit to various audiences worldwide (Exhibit 1.3). The U.S.S.R. and the United States (Voice of America) broadcast the most hours in the most languages (Exhibit 1.4).

B. Surrogate services such as Radio Liberty, Radio Free Europe, and Radio Marti attempt to simulate domestic services within the target countries.

C. Some nations resort to jamming to prevent their citizens from hearing transborder broadcasts.

1.11 U.S. Dominance

A. U.S. policy favors a free flow of communications, but Third World nations, concerned with neocolonialism, question a free flow that runs almost entirely in one direction.

B. A UNESCO-sponsored New World Information Order proposed restrictions on certain kinds of communications. This proposal was vigorously opposed by the United States.

KEY TERMS

Identify or define each of these key terms from Chapter 1.

A. *Indicate the name of each organization.*

1. BBC ______________________________
2. IBA ______________________________
3. ITU ______________________________
4. WARC ______________________________
5. RTL ______________________________
6. USIA ______________________________
7. UNESCO ______________________________

B. *Indicate the target audience for each of the following broadcast services.*

1. Radio Luxembourg ______________________________

2. Radio Liberty ______________________________

3. Radio Free Europe ______________________________

4. Radio Marti ______________________________

5. Radio Moscow ______________________________

6. Eurovision ______________________________

7. Intervision ______________________________

8. Voice of America ______________________________

9. BBC World Service ______________________________

C. *Each of the following political perspectives describes the way different broadcasting systems operate in various countries of the world. After each term, list a country where that political perspective is prevalent and tell how broadcasting in that country is supported financially.*

1. authoritarianism ______________________________

____

2. paternalism ______________________________

____

3. permissivism ______________________________

____

4. pluralism ______________________________

____

D. *How does quantitative audience measurement differ from qualitative audience measurement? (Note that the latter uses such techniques as* appreciation indexes.*) Which countries and systems are most likely to use which types of measurements?*

____

____

E. *How does pirate radio differ from clandestine radio?*

F. *How does jamming differ from transborder interference?*

G. *Who supports and who opposes the New World Information Order?*

H. *Name at least two countries that use receiver licensee fees to support broadcasting. How are these fees collected?*

I. *Define cultural imperialism and Western news values. How are these terms used and by whom?*

J. *Broadcasting is part of a larger concept we call telecommunications. What are some of the nonbroadcasting functions included in this broader term?*

SELF-TEST

Fill in the Blank

1. The authors use the term ______________________ to describe traditional broadcasting services that existed before cable, direct satellite broadcasting, videocassette recorders, and other innovations changed our media environment.

2. When two nearby broadcasters transmit on the same or adjacent frequencies, they create ______________________.

3. Broadcasting systems that give more emphasis to audience wants than to audience needs are called ______________________.

4. Broadcasting systems that give more emphasis to audience needs than to audience wants are called ______________________.

5. With the exception of a few early stations that were established before the rule was made, all radio and television stations east of the Mississippi River must identify themselves with a call sign of ______________________ letters beginning with the letter ______________________. Call signs for stations west of the Mississippi must begin with the letter ______________________.

6. The international broadcaster with the greatest credibility is ______________________.

7. The North American country most concerned about cultural identity is ______________________.

8. The authors refer to Radio Liberty and Radio Free Europe as ______________________ services.

9. In which two countries is "wired radio" used extensively? ______________________

True/False

T F 1. The portable radio you use in the United States could also be used in Europe.

T F 2. The television receiver you use in the United States could also be used in Europe.

T F 3. Third World countries generally apply a pluralistic perspective to their various broadcasting services.

T F 4. The term that best describes broadcasting in the Soviet Union is *paternalism.*

T F 5. AM radio is classified as a common carrier.

T F 6. The BBC formed a popular music network called Radio One to satisfy listeners who had previously listened to illegal pirate stations.

T F 7. Audience surveys that simply count the number of viewers (TV) or listeners (radio) for various programs are called quantitative measurements.

T F 8. Messages about consumer products (commercials) are never carried on Soviet television.

T F 9. The majority of British broadcasters view American broadcasting as a horrible system to be avoided at all costs.

T F 10. Voice of America broadcasts are available on both AM and FM radio for residents of the United States who want to listen.

T F 11. The New World Information Order is a UN document that encourages the free flow of information across international borders.

PROJECT

Borrow the *World Radio/Television Handbook* from your library and determine the number of different broadcasts in various languages provided by the Voice of America, the BBC World Service, and Radio Moscow. If you have access to a shortwave receiver, listen to an English language broadcast from Radio Moscow. Describe the programming you hear, and compare it to your favorite domestic station.

PART 1

Development

CHAPTER 2

The Rise of Radio

CHAPTER FOCUS

This chapter traces the development of radio from the important theoretical paper by physicist James Clerk Maxwell in 1873 through the establishment of national radio networks in 1927. Radio gained national preeminence very quickly. As an information medium, it was an extension of earlier devices (the telegraph and telephone) that had already gained public acceptance. As an entertainment medium, it quickly found the mass audience that had already been cultivated by earlier media (vaudeville, the phonograph, silent movies).

No one person "invented" radio. Many individuals and corporations contributed to its technical, organizational, and financial evolution. Initially, the federal government was reluctant to regulate radio, but as this medium grew it became increasingly clear that regulation was necessary to allocate channels, prevent interference, and safeguard the public interest.

CAPSULE

Main points from each section of Chapter 2 are summarized below.

2.1 Precedents

A. The transition from rural to urban America concentrated people in the cities where they became potential members of a mass audience. Education and the expansion of leisure time gave this audience the ability and the time to seek news and entertainment.

B. Popular newspapers, vaudeville, the phonograph, and silent movies all were developed before the 1920 period and contributed to the concept of mass media and the content of early radio.

2.2 Wire Communication

A. First the telegraph and later the telephone fulfilled a need for land-based point-to-point communication. Underwater cable made point-to-point telegraphic communication between continents possible.

B. Bell secured two key patents for the telephone in 1876 and 1877 but was unable to raise the capital necessary to develop his company. Bell's company passed into the hands of investors who created the American Telephone and Telegraph Company (AT&T).

C. AT&T licensed independent regional operators, installed *long lines* to connect the regional companies, and used the amplification capabilities of Lee de Forest's *Audion* to make long-distance telephone service a reality. AT&T also controlled the manufacturing of telephone equipment through its Western Electric subsidiary and operated as a regulated monopoly. In 1982 AT&T agreed to settle a government antitrust suit by divesting itself of the local companies.

2.3 Big Business and Patents

A. A patent gives an inventor exclusive rights to an invention for a period of 17 years. The inventor may sell or license that patent to other users.

B. Most of the patents that led to the development of radio were eventually controlled by one of three large corporations – AT&T, General Electric, or Westinghouse.

2.4 Invention of the Wireless

A. A Scottish physicist, James Clerk Maxwell, predicted the existence of invisible radiant energy similar to light. Heinrich Hertz, a German experimenter, proved Maxwell's theory by generating and detecting radio energy and measuring its wavelength in the 1880s.

B. Guglielmo Marconi, utilizing the discoveries of Maxwell and Hertz, invented a method to transmit telegraphic signals over radio waves. This invention was called wireless telegraphy or simply *wireless* (Exhibit 2.1).

C. British Marconi was established as a company in 1897 to manufacture wireless equipment and to offer wireless telegraphic service to the public. A U.S. subsidiary, American Marconi, was created in 1899.

D. Initially, the wireless signal was created by a series of electrical sparks. Later, various methods were used to generate a steady signal or *continuous wave*, which allowed transmission of voice and music signals.

E. Early signals were very weak and difficult to detect. Lee de Forest found a way to amplify these incoming signals. He called this invention the *Audion*. We know it today as the three-element electronic vacuum tube, still to be found in older radio and television sets. This electronic tube was the forerunner of today's transistors and silicon chips.

2.5 Initial Development of Wireless Services

A. Ships at sea were the first commercial customers for wireless telegraphy. The *Titanic* disaster in 1912 demonstrated the importance of radiotelegraphy.

B. During World War I, the Navy took control of U.S. radio. Some ten thousand servicemen received wartime training in wireless. These trainees would form the core of operators for radio broadcasting that emerged after the war.

2.6 Experiments with Radiotelephony

A. Reginald Fessenden and Lee de Forest both experimented with the radio transmission of voices and music (Exhibit 2.2). These transmissions, which approximated the kinds of messages that might be transmitted by telephone, were called *radiotelephony*.

B. De Forest used his Audion as an oscillator to generate a radio frequency for the continuous wave transmission that telephony required (Exhibit 2.3).

2.7 Government Monopoly: The Road Not Taken

A. The Navy viewed radio as a maritime service and supported a bill that would make radio a permanent government monopoly. Congress chose instead to return radio to private ownership.

B. Concern was raised over the issue of ownership. American Marconi, a dominant company holding key radio patents, was owned by a foreign corporation. That corporation, British Marconi, agreed to sell the stock in its American subsidiary to General Electric (GE). General Electric created the Radio Corporation of America (RCA). Westinghouse and AT&T joined GE as investors in RCA.

C. No single company held enough patents to fully develop radio. RCA and its principal investors (GE, Westinghouse, and AT&T) agreed to various cross-licensing agreements in a patent pool that allowed each company to use the patents held by the other companies.

2.8 The "First" Broadcast Station

A. Westinghouse saw a potential market in the sale of factory-built radio receivers. The company recognized that more radios might be sold if programs were available for those who might purchase these receivers (Exhibit 2.4A).

B. Westinghouse created KDKA in 1920 to provide the first organized program service. The company did not sell advertising but rather bore the expense of the station as a means of promoting radio receiver sales (Exhibits 2.4B and 2.5).

2.9 Radio Broadcasting vs. Radiotelephony

A. Two New York radio stations represented opposing philosophies of broadcasting. WJZ, owned initially by Westinghouse and later by RCA, operated as a sales-promotion device to stimulate the sale of receivers. WEAF, owned by AT&T, operated as a message delivery service.

B. The AT&T station leased broadcast time to advertisers who used that time to deliver messages to anyone listening to the station. AT&T provided no programming; that was up to the advertiser. AT&T called this philosophy *toll* broadcasting, the name being derived from toll telephones that required the sender rather than the receiver to pay for the message.

C. The telephone company used its long-distance lines to interconnect a *chain* or network of radio stations (called the *Telephone Group*) in several cities.

D. AT&T, by exercising a clause in its cross-licensing agreement, tried to prevent other stations from selling advertising time. It also refused to interconnect stations owned by RCA, Westinghouse, and GE (the *Radio Group*).

E. Worried about charges of monopoly, AT&T agreed to a revision in the cross-licensing agreement. AT&T would no longer be directly involved in broadcasting but would provide interconnection to any stations willing to pay for the service. The telephone company sold WEAF and all its other broadcasting assets to the Radio Group.

2.10 Evolution of Radio

A. In 1926 the Radio Group created a new subsidiary, the National Broadcasting Company (NBC) to operate a broadcasting *network*. The next year NBC organized two semi-autonomous networks, the Blue network which included stations in the old Radio Group and the Red network which included those stations that had been in the Telephone Group.

B. Another network, CBS, was organized in 1927 and purchased by William Paley a year later. Paley agreed to provide free programming to his affiliate stations and to pay the stations for those hours when the network aired commercials. In exchange, the stations agreed to give CBS the option to buy additional time as needed.

C. Some concern about the exploitation of radio as an advertising medium persisted, but, by 1927, advertising was accepted as the principal form of financial support. Advertising agencies increased their role in broadcasting by becoming the producers of many sponsored programs.

2.11 Government Regulation

A. The Radio Act of 1912, not designed to cover broadcasting, granted radio licenses to all applicants and, as the number of stations grew, interference became a serious problem (Exhibit 2.6).

B. In the *Zenith* decision (1926), a court ruled that the federal government did not have authority under then-existing law to regulate the frequency or power that a broadcaster could use. Broadcasters were free to change frequency and power at will. Interference became even worse, and the sale of radio receivers declined.

C. Broadcasters urged the government to provide regulation and Congress passed the Radio Act of 1927. The act created a Federal Radio Commission (FRC) to license broadcasters and bring order to the airwaves.

KEY TERMS AND NAMES

A. *For each of the following inventions, name the person credited.*

1. the telegraph ______________________________

2. the telephone ______________________________

3. the phonograph ______________________________

4. the Audion ______________________________

B. *For each of the following achievements, name the person credited.*

1. predicted the existence of invisible radiant energy ______________________________

2. generated radio energy and measured its wavelength ______________________________

3. first to offer wireless telegraphic service to the public ______________________________

4. wireless operator who provided information about the *Titanic* disaster ______________________________

____

5. first to use radiotelephony and to broadcast ______________________

6. chairman of General Electric whose negotiations created a new company __________

____

7. Westinghouse engineer whose transmissions led to the first radio station __________

____

8. purchased and strengthened the unstable radio network that eventually became CBS

____

9. convener of the First Radio Conference in 1922 ______________________

10. evangelist whose radio station demonstrated the need for government regulation

____

C. *Identify these stations, networks, corporations, or agencies.*

1. the British news agency ______________________

2. two American news agencies ______________________ and __________

____

3. the French news agency ______________________

4. the Soviet news agency ______________________

5. the regulated monopoly that pioneered long-distance telephony ______________

6. held a monopoly position in telegraphy ______________________

7. manufacturer of telephones and other equipment for AT&T ______________

8. first to manufacture light bulbs and owner of a group of pioneer radio stations ________

____

9. another electrical giant and owner of the oldest radio station ______________

10. parent company of American Marconi ______________________

11. company that took over the activities of American Marconi ______________________

12. amateur radiotelephone station operated by Westinghouse ______________________

13. oldest radio station still in operation ______________________

14. the initials that apply to tuning signals from distant radio stations ______________

15. early New York flagship station of the Radio Group ______________________

16. early New York flagship station of the Telephone Group ______________________

17. first company organized to operate a network ______________________

18. semiautonomous network created from Radio Group stations ______________________

19. semiautonomous network created from Telephone Group stations ______________

____

20. network that began as United Independent Broadcasters ______________________

21. agency created by Congress to supervise and regulate the airwaves ______________

D. *Supply the correct term for each of the following definitions.*

1. theatrical acts popular during the 1880–1920 period that established the pattern for later radio programming ______________________

2. early motion picture camera developed by Edison ______________________

3. a system for translating the letters of the alphabet into patterns of electrical impulses

____

4. the key element in the telephone that converts sound energy into electrical energy

____

5. gives the holder exclusive property rights to an invention for a period of 17 years

____

6. an early term for the radio transmission of telegraph signals ____________

7. kind of transmitted signal necessary to transmit voice and music ____________

8. a generator built by GE to supply continuous high-frequency radio energy ____________

____

9. a later and improved signal generator that utilized even higher frequencies ____________

____

10. two solid-state successors to the electronic vacuum tube ____________

11. gradual weakening of an electronic signal over distance ____________

12. problem created when two stations broadcast on the same frequency ____________

____

E. *Explain how radiotelegraphy differs from radiotelephony.*

____

____

____

____

____

SELF-TEST

Fill in the Blank

1. Newspapers, magazines, radio, television, and other means of communication that appeal to mass audiences are collectively referred to as the ____________.

2. The power of wireless telegraphy to communicate in time of crisis was dramatically illustrated after the sinking of the ____________.

3. The term ______________________________ was used to describe AT&T's philosophy that the sender of a radio message should pay for the service.

4. The term ______________________________ was used to describe the first radio networks.

5. Individual stations that belong to and receive programs from a network are called ____________

______________________________.

6. The judicial event that demonstrated the weakness of the Radio Act of 1912 was known as

the ______________________________.

7. As a result of the above event, Congress passed the ______________________________ which established a governmental agency to regulate broadcasting.

True/False

T **F** 1. The first mass medium to have a significant impact on the American public was radio.

T **F** 2. Alexander Graham Bell lacked the capital to develop his invention and subsequently lost control of his own patent.

T **F** 3. Under government-imposed divestiture, AT&T separated itself from the local operating companies but continued to own and operate Western Electric and Bell Laboratories.

T **F** 4. A radio wave with a frequency of 100 cycles per second would be expressed as 100 HZ.

T **F** 5. The principal value of the Audion was its ability to amplify a signal.

T **F** 6. Guglielmo Marconi was the first to transmit a radiotelephony broadcast.

T **F** 7. Radio Corporation of America (RCA) was formed primarily because the U.S. government was opposed to a foreign-owned company controlling important radio patents.

T **F** 8. Westinghouse-owned KDKA was the first station to carry advertising.

T **F** 9. AT&T-owned WEAF was the first station to provide programming for the enjoyment of its listeners.

T **F** 10. Initially, AT&T refused to provide network interconnection for Radio Group stations, thereby forcing these stations to use the telegraph wires of Western Union.

T **F** 11. Later, AT&T decided to cease its direct involvement in radio and sold its stations to RCA.

T **F** 12. After institutional or good-will advertising was successfully utilized on radio in 1922, broadcasters were quick to move to direct advertising that emphasized selling points unique to the products involved.

T **F** 13. The Radio Act of 1912 directed the secretary of commerce and labor to grant broadcast licenses to all who applied.

T **F** 14. At each of four national radio conferences, broadcasters declared their intention to adopt industrial self-government as a means of avoiding government regulation.

T **F** 15. The Federal Radio Commission was initially established as a temporary agency but was later made a permanent body by Congress.

PROJECT

Select and read a biography or autobiography about Guglielmo Marconi, Lee de Forest, Reginald Fessenden, David Sarnoff, William Paley, or any of the other radio pioneers mentioned in this chapter. (See bibliography in text for suggestions.) What characteristics describe such industry pioneers? How do they compare with technical and business leaders of today?

CHAPTER 3

From Radio to Television

CHAPTER FOCUS

Chapter 3 examines the radio industry during its peak years as the principal home entertainment medium until eclipsed by television in the early 1950s. Television itself was delayed by World War II, but once it was introduced the medium grew quickly in terms of stations, audience size, and network programming capability. Radio survived as a secondary medium, reverting to inexpensive local programming that emphasized recorded music, news, and talk. FM radio, which had largely been ignored in the 1940s and 1950s, was more favorably received in the 1960s and 1970s and eventually surpassed AM radio in terms of audience size.

CAPSULE

Main points from each section of Chapter 3 are summarized below.

3.1 Radio During the Great Depression (1929–1937)

A. Radio prospered during the Depression for three reasons. First, the public turned increasingly to radio as a form of free entertainment during a grim period. Second, talent turned to radio when opportunities in vaudeville and theater dried up. Third, companies turned to radio sponsorship as a way of retaining and building a clientele for their products (Exhibit 3.1).

B. Overall, radio programming was quite conservative, but some free speech exploiters incurred regulatory action by placing personal gain ahead of the public interest.

C. NBC retained dominance during this period with CBS a strong second and the newly formed Mutual Broadcasting System (1934) a weak third.

3.2 Radio Controversies

A. Copyright law requires broadcasters to pay a performing right when copyrighted music is played. The National Association of Broadcasters (NAB) was formed (1923) to negotiate with the American Society of Composers, Authors, and Publishers (ASCAP). When ASCAP proposed a substantial fee increase in 1940, the broadcasters formed Broadcast Music Incorporated (BMI).

B. Newspapers, fearing competition, attempted to limit the quantity and quality of news made available to radio by the newspaper-controlled wire services. These efforts were only briefly successful and eroded in the late 1930s.

3.3 Television and FM Radio

A. Experimental mechanical television systems were demonstrated in the 1920s. The BBC offered the first high-definition (405 lines) television to the general public in 1936. RCA demonstrated a 441-line experimental system at the 1939 World's Fair. In 1941 the FCC approved the NTSC-recommended standard of 525 lines and 30 frames-per-second which is still in effect today.

B. Frequency modulation (FM), patented in 1933 by Edwin Armstrong, was largely ignored for two reasons (Exhibit 3.4). First, RCA, the dominant electronics firm, gave priority to television. Second, FM threatened the profitability of the already developed AM system. After World War II, many AM broadcasters did obtain FM licenses but chose to simulcast their AM and FM programming.

C. Networks initially scorned recorded programming but slowly changed their position with the arrival of improved recording techniques. These included audio tape recorders as well as 33 $\frac{1}{3}$ and 45 rpm records.

3.4 Broadcasting at War (1938–1946)

A. Even though consumer products were scarce, manufacturers continued to advertise on radio to keep brand names before the public.

B. European correspondents, led by Edward R. Murrow, set a high standard for reporting during this period that established the CBS network as the leader in broadcast journalism (see Box in Chapter 3).

C. Six experimental TV stations broadcast civil defense programs during the war. In 1945, the FCC reaffirmed the NTSC 525-line standard, thereby setting the stage for the postwar growth of television.

3.5 Radio Networks: Development and Decline

A. The FCC "Chain Broadcasting Regulations" required NBC to sell one of its two networks. The weaker Blue network, sold in 1943, became ABC in 1945. The rules also freed stations from the option-time restrictions in their network affiliation contracts by giving them the right to reject (pre-empt) network programs.

B. William Paley made CBS the dominant radio network by persuading Jack Benny and other radio stars to leave NBC in the late 1940s and come to CBS.

C. ABC merged with Paramount Theaters to gain financial support and improve its competitive position in television with NBC and CBS. Mutual acquired many smaller stations as affiliates but still remained a distant fourth in terms of radio audience.

3.6 Television at Last

A. The FCC, overwhelmed by applicants for the 12 VHF television channels then available, imposed a freeze that lasted four years while it studied the situation. During this period, the 108 prefreeze stations had an enviable monopoly.

B. In 1952 the FCC issued its *Sixth Report and Order*, ending the freeze. The 12 existing VHF channels were supplemented with 70 new UHF channels. Some channels were reserved for noncommercial, educational (public) use. This report established the allotment pattern for television channels on a market-by-market basis. The ruling, though amended many times, is still in effect today (Exhibit 3.5).

C. The FCC decision to *intermix* VHF and UHF assignments in the same market created a serious disadvantage for UHF stations that could only be received by those TV sets with converters and had much less range than VHF. Legislation passed in 1962, effective 1964, required manufacturers to produce all-channel receivers. Still later, click-stop tuning was required for both UHF and VHF.

D. The CBS incompatible color system initially approved by the FCC in 1950 was set aside in favor of an RCA color system compatible with existing black-and-white receivers. Initially, color receivers were expensive and only NBC produced programs in color.

3.7 The TV Age Begins

A. The major radio networks (except Mutual) immediately assumed a leading role in television. AT&T completed a coaxial cable and microwave relay system in 1951 that linked the country and made possible national network programming.

B. Initially, all TV programming was live because videotape recording had not yet been invented. Early TV programs had single sponsors and emphasized original drama that appealed to wealthier families who could afford expensive TV receivers.

C. NBC's Sylvester ("Pat") Weaver introduced segmented sponsorship that allowed more advertisers to participate in this increasingly expensive medium. He also introduced one-time specials.

D. William Paley, CBS's master programmer, made his network the ratings leader in 1955, and CBS remained number one for 21 successive years.

E. ABC, a distant third in ratings, gave more attention to the demographic composition (young, urban) of its audience.

F. DuMont, a weak fourth TV network, ceased to operate in 1955.

G. Videotape recording, successfully demonstrated by Ampex in 1956, soon brought an end to the "live decade." Traditional film production techniques were adapted to television as the production of most prime-time television programs moved from New York and Chicago to Los Angeles.

3.8 Radio Responds to Television

A. Radio network programming declined after 1950 as the stars moved to television. Networks scaled down service to hourly news bulletins and short features. Individual stations substituted music to fill the majority of air time.

B. Postwar growth in the number of radio stations, together with declining revenue for radio as a whole, brought a drastic reduction in individual station earnings for several years.

C. Many radio stations turned to a rock music format or top-40 programming in the mid-1950s in an attempt to win a particular segment of the radio audience.

D. Public interest in hi-fi sound and FCC standards for FM stereo (1961) brought a new attention to this form of radio. A 1964 FCC nonduplication rule forced major market stations to reduce simulcasting and program their AM and FM stations independently at least 50 percent of the time. FM audience size grew dramatically during the 1960s and 1970s and by the mid-1980s exceeded the audience for AM radio.

3.9 Ethical Crises

A. High-stakes TV quiz shows captured audiences, but the public was shocked to learn the shows were rigged. Congress belatedly made such rigging illegal (Exhibit 3.9).

B. Political *blacklisting*, an outgrowth of the Cold War period, was timidly accepted by networks and advertising agencies. Many unjustly accused radio and TV performers became unemployable. Edward R. Murrow devoted a *See It Now* documentary to *McCarthyism.*

C. Two FCC commissioners were forced to resign in the late 1950s after investigations revealed that one had taken a bribe and the other had engaged in illegal billing for official travel.

KEY TERMS AND NAMES

A. *For each of the following inventions, name the peson credited.*

1. the mechanical scanning disc that separated a visual scene into individual lines of information ______________________
2. an early mechanical system for transmitting "radiomovies" ______________________
3. a 30-line, mechanically scanned TV system used in Britain ______________________
4. an improved electronic scanning system with a supressed retrace pattern and synchronizing pulses ______________________
5. an electronic camera pickup tube, the iconoscope ______________________
6. FM radio ______________________
7. the $33\frac{1}{3}$ LP record ______________________

B. *Name the person credited with the following programming innovations.*

1. created advertising copy written for radio rather than print ______________________
2. presented the first regularly scheduled nightly newscast on NBC ______________________
3. first radio star to move from real-time to recorded programs ______________________
4. director and performer in *The War of the Worlds* ______________________

5. radio's two best-known playwrights ______________________________

6. prominent war correspondent later known for *See It Now* documentaries

____

7. pioneer radio commentator remembered for his coverage of the Munich crisis

____

8. innovative NBC-TV programming vice president ______________________________

9. radio disc jockey who gave rock music its name ______________________________

10. quiz show contestant who first gained fame and then notoriety ____________________

11. AFTRA officer and victim of blacklisting ______________________________

C. *Other names from the chapter.*

1. bogus physician who used the public airwaves for his own purposes

____

2. Catholic priest with charismatic radio appeal and pro-Nazi sympathies

____

3. long-time president of the American Federation of Musicians and opponent of recorded music ______________________________

4. radio newscaster and head of the Office of War Information ____________________

5. electronics manufacturer who founded a short-lived television network

____

6. politician notorious for character assassinations based on unfounded accusations of Communist sympathies ______________________________

D. *Identify the stations, networks, or organizations.*

1. network created to allow stations to exchange programs ______________________
2. the first music-licensing organization ______________________
3. music-licensing organization initially formed by broadcasters ______________________
4. organization of broadcast stations initially formed to negotiate music-licensing agreements but now also active as an industry lobby ______________________
5. wire service established to provide copy to radio stations for limited, twice-daily news summaries ______________________
6. government organization that created the Voice of America ______________________
7. successor to the NBC Blue Network ______________________
8. flagship station of this new network ______________________
9. fourth television network that lasted for nine years ______________________
10. electronics firm that developed videotape recording ______________________
11. first TV production company to move to Hollywood and produce programs on film ______________________
12. self-appointed blacklist group that offered to clear the names of those accused of Communist leanings if certain circumstances were met ______________________

SELF-TEST

Fill in the Blank

1. Phrase used to describe President Franklin D. Roosevelt's radio addresses to the public.

____

2. One of the most popular radio programs of the 1930s, although racist by today's standards.

   ____

3. Name of the organization that set standards for television that were approved by the FCC in 1941 and are still in use today. ______________________________

4. Term used to describe the practice of broadcasting the same programming on co-owned AM and FM stations. ______________________________

5. Radio drama that simulated a newscast and frightened a sizable segment of the audience.

   ____

6. FCC regulations that gave stations rather than networks the final determination of programming to be aired. ______________________________

7. FCC order that created the UHF-band, educational, noncommercial stations and a nationwide channel allotment plan. ______________________________

8. The radio format that appealed to youthful audiences by emphasizing a limited number of records. ______________________________

9. Developed by Bell Laboratories, this small substitute for the vacuum tube gave its name to a new generation of pocket radios. ______________________________

10. The term used to describe a period in American history when concern about Communism reached epidemic proportions and many were unjustly accused of disloyalty.

    ____

True/False

T F 1. Businesses were reluctant to spend money on radio advertising during the Depression; networks were forced to air a greater proportion of sustaining programs than during the previous period.

T F 2. The National Association of Broadcasters was formed so that broadcasters could present a united front when dealing with ASCAP.

T F 3. The engineering standards used in American television today are the same ones approved by the FCC in 1941.

T F 4. Radio advertising declined during World War II because manufacturers were involved in military production and only a limited quantity of consumer goods was available.

T F 5. CBS's leadership in news can be traced to its *World News Round-up* and similar programs that began in 1938 and continued through World War II.

T F 6. The FCC's "Chain Broadcasting Regulations" led eventually to the creation of ABC.

T F 7. Channel 1 was originally assigned to television but reassigned to land mobile communications in 1948 because of interference problems.

T F 8. The UHF band was a direct result of the FCC's historic *Sixth Report and Order.*

T F 9. Incompatible color existed with FCC approval until the Korean War.

T F 10. NBC was the network leader in color production primarily because RCA, its parent corporation, hoped to profit from the sale of color receivers.

T F 11. During television's first decade most of the programs were produced on motion picture film.

T F 12. Early network television programs were usually single-sponsor shows.

T F 13. The first network to recognize the importance of demographics was ABC.

T F 14. As the audience for television surpassed that of radio, the number of radio stations declined.

T F 15. The FCC contributed greatly to FM radio's success by implementing a nonduplication rule.

T F 16. AM stereo, although it came much later than FM stereo, has been just as successful in increasing audience size and loyalty.

T F 17. The rigging of quiz shows, while clearly unethical, is not illegal today.

T F 18. The broadcasting industry supported blacklisting because industry executives believed various anticommunist groups were sincere and patriotic in their efforts to cleanse broadcasting of subversive elements.

PROJECT

Locate and listen to recordings of some of the programs from radio's "golden age." These tapes and records are widely available in record stores and audio libraries. Try to locate some radio soap operas and note how they compare with present-day television soaps. If you live in the New York City area, visit the Museum of Broadcasting where you can not only listen to vintage radio but also view early television programs.

CHAPTER 4

Era of Electronic Media

CHAPTER FOCUS

During the 1970s and 1980s, traditional television and radio were augmented by a variety of newer program distribution systems. Two of the most significant are cable television and videocassette recorders. Not all of the technological innovations have proven economically viable, however. Some have already been abandoned by their corporate creators. Others are still in the market experimentation stage.

Public broadcasting emerged as an alternative to commercial broadcasting during this period and also was the first to move from landline to satellite distribution of network programming. Changing political philosophy caused the FCC to adopt a deregulatory posture and to encourage greater competition between traditional broadcasters and those utilizing alternative delivery systems.

CAPSULE

Main points from each section of Chapter 4 are summarized below.

4.1 The Limits of Television

A. Both allotment patterns and geographic factors limit the number of television signals readily available to many Americans.

B. Boosters and translators are used in mountainous states to retransmit signals into areas with poor television reception.

4.2 Rise of Cable Television

A. Cable television, initially called community antenna television or CATV, performed a retransmission function.

B. Cable began in small towns. Later, the industry expanded to larger cities with more potential subscribers.

C. As cable developed, systems began to increase the number of channels available to subscribers. They imported distant signals, originated some programs locally, and added movie and sports channels.

D. Because cable offers subscribers a greater choice of channels, it fragments the audience, thereby reducing the number of people available to view each local broadcast station.

E. Because cable operators ran cable over public property, they were licensed or "franchised" by municipal governments.

F. The FCC, fearing that cable might weaken the economic support system of local stations (advertising revenue based on audience size), created regulations that mandated some cable activities and limited others.

G. In 1977 a federal appeals court ruled that the FCC had erred in treating cable as a supplement to—rather than the equal of—broadcast television.

H. Both this ruling and a changing political philosophy led to deregulation and the view that the FCC should encourage broadcasters and cable operators to compete rather than attempt to protect the former from the latter (Exhibit 4.1).

4.3 The Cable Establishment

A. Both domestic satellites (domsats) and inexpensive television receive-only antennas (TVROs) were developed during the 1970s (Exhibit 4.2). These two innovations significantly reduced the cost of distributing television signals.

B. HBO (1975) and Turner Broadcasting System leased satellite transponders to distribute their signals to thousands of cable systems. Turner's Atlanta station WTBS became the first superstation (1976) to have a sizable audience beyond its broadcast signal coverage.

C. Warner-Amex developed Qube to demonstrate the potential for interactive cable television. The system, although technically feasible, was not economically viable and was eventually terminated.

4.4 Pay Television

A. Some limited experimentation with over-the-air subscription (pay) television took place during the 1950s, but the results were inconclusive.

B. After the FCC removed restrictive rules, a number of major market UHF stations began in 1977 to broadcast a scrambled signal to pay television subscribers. These single-channel services could not, however, compete with the multichannel services available from cable systems (Exhibit 4.3).

C. Multipoint Distribution Service (MDS) also broadcast movies and other programming services to subscribers in major cities. Additional channels from the little-used Instructional Television Fixed Service (ITFS) band have been given to MDS operators who now offer multichannel MDS or MMDS (Exhibit 4.4).

D. Satellite Master Antenna Television (SMATV) is an alternative delivery system suitable for large building complexes. It provides a service similar to cable, but, because all equipment is on private property, no municipal franchise is required nor do FCC regulations apply (Exhibit 4.5).

4.5 Traditional Broadcasting

A. The number of radio and television stations continued to grow during the 1970s and 1980s although at a slower rate than during the 1950s and 1960s.

B. ABC gained strength in programming and management and achieved parity with CBS and NBC in the 1970s.

C. An FCC inquiry in 1980 concluded that dominance by three networks was more a result of television channel allotments than of monopolistic practices by ABC, NBC, and CBS. It suggested that competing delivery systems would lessen the dominance of these three networks in the future.

4.6 Public Broadcasting

A. The Public Broadcasting Act of 1967 established a Corporation for Public Broadcasting (CPB) to create public television and radio networks and to transmit federal funding to individual stations. The Public Broadcasting System (PBS) was created to interconnect the approximately 280 television stations. National Public Radio (NPR) was created to interconnect and produce some of the programming for some 200 of the larger radio stations.

B. In 1978 PBS became the first broadcast interconnection to switch from landlines to satellite. NPR made a similar move in 1980. ABC, NBC, and CBS began conversion to satellite delivery a few years later.

4.7 Home Video Center

A. Sony introduced the U-matic videocassette recorder intended for the educational and business market in 1972. The Betamax VCR created for home use followed in 1975. A second home-use VCR, the VHS system, was introduced in 1977 (Exhibit 4.6).

B. Consumer videodisc systems were marketed by Magnavox and RCA. These machines and the individual discs were initially cheaper than their VCR counterparts. Videodiscs can only play back prerecorded material. As the price gap between VCRs and videodiscs narrowed, the market for videodisc systems declined and RCA abandoned the market in 1984.

C. As the number of VCR households grew, prerecorded materials were less frequently purchased and more frequently rented. Video rental stores appeared almost overnight in shopping malls. Consumers also used their VCRs for timeshifting, recording broadcast programs for viewing at a time of their choosing (Exhibit 4.7).

4.8 Developments to Come

A. Both teletext and videotex appear as pages of print on the TV screen. Teletext is carried as a part of the broadcast signal although special decoders are needed to retrieve the data. Videotex is a separate signal transmitted by cable or by telephone wires (Exhibit 4.8).

B. Direct broadcast satellite (DBS) provides a direct link between the program supplier and the television viewer (Exhibit 4.9). One attempt was made to establish a DBS system that would supply programming to rural homes too isolated to be served by cable. This system had few subscribers and failed. The outlook for DBS development in the United States is bleak although DBS may be more successful in Europe.

C. An experimental, high-definition television system has been developed by Sony that would substitute a 1125-line picture for the 525-line picture in effect since 1941. Problems of compatibility with existing broadcast transmitters and home receivers have not been resolved.

D. Stereo television was successfully introduced during the 1984–85 television season.

KEY TERMS

A. *Identify the following acronyms by giving each one its full title.*

1. CATV ______
2. TVRO ______
3. HBO ______
4. STV ______
5. MDS ______
6. MMDS ______
7. ITFS ______
8. SMATV ______
9. CPB ______
10. PBS ______
11. NPR ______
12. VCR ______
13. DBS ______
14. HDTV ______

B. *Supply the correct term for each of the following.*

1. used in mountainous areas to strengthen a weak TV signal ______
2. used to retransmit signals over a different frequency ______
3. describes a delivery system that uses the creation of someone else without contributing to the profitability of the product ______
4. licenses granted by municipal governments to cable television operators ______

5. a cable augmentation service that supplies nonbroadcast programming at no cost to subscribers ______

6. FCC rule that requires cable carriage of local TV stations ______

7. cable channels available to government entities, educational institutions, and the general public ______

8. Westar I was the first ______

9. that part of a satellite that receives a signal from an earth station and retransmits it to other earth stations ______

10. a station whose signal is distributed by cable and, consequently, has an audience beyond its usual geographic coverage ______

11. technique used in pay television to limit reception to paying customers ______

12. electronic appliance that gives the TV viewer a greater choice of what to watch and when to watch it ______

13. electronic appliance unable to retain its sales appeal because of its limited function as a playback unit ______

14. viewing TV programs at other than their broadcast time ______

15. printed pages coded within a television signal ______

16. printed pages carried over a cable or telephone line ______

17. improvement in TV sound first used in the 1984-1985 season ______

C. *Supply a name for each of the following.*

1. TV station owner who used satellite and cable to expand the audience

______

2. call letters of the TV station known as "super 17" ______________________

3. interactive cable system that was a technical success but an economic failure

____

4. videocassette format developed by Sony for business use ______________________

5. videocassette format developed by Sony for consumer use ______________________

6. rival VCR format developed for consumer use ______________________

SELF-TEST

Fill in the Blank

1. When cable increases viewer choice, it ______________________ audiences and leaves local broadcast stations with lower ratings and less appeal to advertisers.

2. Initially, HBO used microwave relay to distribute its programs to cable operators. In 1975, it switched to ______________________ distribution.

3. Cable systems that permit viewers to send data "upstream" to the cable company are said to be ______________________.

4. SMATV is popular with apartment building owners because it is not ______________________ by any level of government.

5. Corporate donations to public broadcasting that cover the full or partial cost of specific programs are called ______________________.

6. Although movies and other prerecorded materials may be purchased for use with a VCR, most consumers prefer to ______________________ the cassettes.

True/False

T F 1. During the 1950s and 1960s, most homes could receive only three to five television channels.

T F 2. Cable television began in New York City where tall buildings made it difficult for television set owners to pick up an adequate over-the-air signal.

T F 3. Most of the initial regulation of the cable industry by the FCC was designed to protect broadcasting.

T F 4. HBO is a "pay-per-view" rather than a "pay-per-channel" service.

T F 5. The Warner-Amex Qube system initially built in Columbus, Ohio, has been successfully adopted in many other markets.

T F 6. Over-the-air pay television has not been successful because it offers subscribers only one channel.

T F 7. Because MDS is a common carrier, the holder of the license must assume responsibility for programming the service.

T F 8. After a lengthy investigation, the FCC concluded that ABC, NBC, and CBS had engaged in monopolistic practices to prevent the formation of a fourth network.

T F 9. AM stereo has been slow to develop, in part, because the FCC refused to set a technical standard for this medium.

T F 10. Members of the board of directors of the Corporation for Public Broadcasting are appointed by the president of the United States.

T F 11. CBS was the first television network to utilize satellite transmission rather than landlines for the distribution of network programs to affiliate stations.

T F 12. Videodiscs have greater appeal with consumers than do videocassettes.

T F 13. Teletext and videotex use television sets with special decoders to deliver print and graphic materials to potential users.

T F 14. DBS is an example of "too much technology chasing too few audience dollars."

T F 15. Since 1970, the FCC has demonstrated a preference for marketplace rather than government control of both traditional broadcasting and many of the newer developments in telecommunications.

PROJECT

Locate and visit a cable television system. Most cable systems maintain their offices, their local origination and public access studios, and their engineering equipment (the headend) in the same location. Ask what channels are provided to cable subscribers and how the programming for these channels is received by the cable system.

PART 2

Technology

CHAPTER 5

Basic Physical Concepts

CHAPTER FOCUS

Radio and television, more than other mass media, are dependent on the physical laws of nature. The broadcast signal is a radio wave that performs a particular function in a highly predictable manner. This chapter explains the physical characteristics of radio. Please note that the term *radio* is used both here and in the text to refer not just to sound broadcasting, but to all forms of wireless communication.

CAPSULE

Main points from each section of Chapter 5 are summarized below.

5.1 Electromagnetic Spectrum

A. Radio is a form of energy that travels at a velocity of 186,000 miles or 300 million meters per second. Radio waves, like visible light, x-rays, and other forms of electromagnetic energy, travel in an oscillating motion.

B. All forms of electromagnetic energy can be described in terms of both frequency and wavelength. The number of oscillations per second is the frequency and the distance between oscillations is the wavelength.

C. Radio waves have relatively low frequencies and are at the lower end of the electromagnetic spectrum (Exhibit 5.1). Visible light has higher frequencies. Cosmic rays have the highest frequencies and are at the upper end of the spectrum.

D. Frequencies toward the lower end of the spectrum are generally easier to use for radio communications. At higher frequencies, the wavelength becomes shorter and the radio waves behave more like light—they are limited to line-of-sight distances.

5.2 Sound Waves

A. Sound energy is both similar to and different from electromagnetic energy. While sound waves oscillate in the same manner as radio waves, sound waves travel at a much lower velocity (Exhibit 5.2).

B. Sound waves have amplitude, length, frequency, and velocity. Each sound wave has a positive and a negative phase. When two waves of equal amplitude are in phase, the resulting amplitude is doubled. When two waves of equal amplitude are out of phase, the resulting amplitude is reduced or canceled out entirely. All of this contributes to the quality of broadcast sound.

C. A pure tone has only one frequency. For example, middle C is 264 hertz. Most sounds consist of many different frequencies with varying amplitudes. The lower frequencies, called *fundamentals*, give sounds their pitch. The higher frequencies, called *overtones* or *harmonics*, give sounds their distinctive quality (Exhibit 5.3).

5.3 Radio Waves

A. Radio waves, like sound waves, lose amplitude or strength as they travel. Like sound waves, they can be absorbed or reflected. Radio waves do not need to travel in an atmosphere such as air. They actually travel best in a vacuum.

B. Radio waves travel at a fixed velocity. Frequency and wavelength vary. Because velocity (300 million meters per second) is the product of frequency times wavelength, the relationship between frequency and wavelength is inverse. As one increases, the other decreases.

C. A radio wave can be identified by either its frequency or its wavelength. A radio wave with a frequency of 60,000 hertz, (600 kHz on an AM radio) has a wavelength of 500 meters. Conversely, a radio wave with a frequency of 120,000 hertz, (1200 kHz on an AM radio) has a wavelength of 250 meters.

D. A broadcast transmitter generates radio energy at the station's allotted frequency. This radio signal is called a *carrier wave* and can be said to "carry" the broadcast or other signal.

5.4 Modulation

A. The basic *carrier wave* carries no information until it is modulated. The process of modulation places an intended signal (a meaningful series of amplitude or frequency patterns) on the carrier wave.

B. Modulation involves frequencies above and below the carrier wave. These frequencies are called sidebands. The number of frequencies in both sidebands determines the bandwidth and thus, to some extent, sound quality.

C. These frequencies are called a channel. Channels used to transmit very simple information such as telegraphy require very little bandwidth. Channels used to transmit highly complex information such as color television require a great deal of bandwidth: they must be able to move many individual bits of information.

D. Information can be placed on a carrier wave by modulating either the amplitude (AM) or the frequency (FM)–(Exhibits 5.5 and 5.6). Television uses both methods, AM for the video signal and FM for the audio signal.

5.5 Digital Signal Processing

A. AM and FM signals are called analogue patterns because their shapes are analogous to the wave forms of the original signal. Digital signal processing employs the *binary code* used by computers to quantify information into a series of numbers consisting of the digits 0 and 1 (Exhibit 5.7).

B. Digitized signals are protected from the many forms of distortion that affect analogue signals.

C. In digital signal processing, the number of on-and-off signals or *bits* a channel can handle per second becomes the measure of the channel's information carrying capacity. Complex information requires a very high bit speed that, in turn, requires great bandwidth.

D. Currently, digital signal processing is used only in the prebroadcasting phases of production, not in the transmission and reception of radio signals.

5.6 Wave Propagation

A. Radio waves may radiate in all directions from a transmitting antenna, but many different factors determine the distance and shape of the coverage area. One of these factors is the frequency of the radio wave.

B. Radio waves in and above the VHF band follow a straight path (called "line of sight") to the horizon. These are called *direct waves.* Radio waves in and below the MF band follow the curvature of the earth and travel beyond the horizon. These are called *ground waves* (Exhibit 5.8).

C. Radio waves in the MF and HF bands also radiate upward into the atmosphere. Some of these waves encounter the ionosphere and are refracted back to earth. These *sky waves* may then bounce off the surface of the earth and back to the ionosphere where the process might be repeated. MF signals (AM radio) are affected by this sky-wave phenomenon only at night. HF signals (short-wave international radio) are subject to the sky-wave phenomenon at all times (Exhibit 5.9).

5.7 Antennas

A. The length of a transmitting antenna is mathematically related to the wavelength of the signal it radiates. Antenna radiating elements are usually one-half or one-quarter the length of the carrier wave (Exhibit 5.10).

B. AM transmitting antennas are placed in areas of good ground conductivity.

C. FM and TV antennas are placed on mountain tops or on tall buildings to maximize their range by extending their line of sight.

D. Shortwave antennas are very complex because international broadcasting uses many different frequencies and each frequency requires its own antenna.

E. Most AM and some FM stations use directional antennas to maximize their effectiveness and to avoid interference with other stations.

5.8 Spectrum Conservation

A. Through the International Telecommunication Union (ITU), national authorities cooperate on a worldwide division of the electromagnetic spectrum. Various segments (bands) of the spectrum are *allocated* for different services.

B. Allocation is based on existing services, on the needs of the new service, and on the appropriate propagation characteristics of the various frequencies.

C. Frequency allocations must be made for services other than broadcasting such as police, fire, taxicab, and satellite services.

D. Multiplexing, the transmission of two or more independent signals on the same channel, is used to conserve frequencies, transmit stereo, and for other purposes. Band compression, the selective omission of repetitive information, is another method used to reduce the need for spectrum frequencies.

KEY TERMS

A. *Each of the following terms relates to radio waves.*

1. term used to describe the vibrating or alternating motion of radio waves ____________
2. the number of times per second a radio wave vibrates ____________
3. when a radio wave loses strength, it is said to ____________
4. a complete wave consists of two ____________
5. the speed or ____________ of a radio wave is 186,000 miles/second
6. as frequency decreases, ____________ increases
7. term used to describe all radio waves arranged in the order of their frequencies ____________

B. *More information about radio waves*

1. international term that means one cycle per second ____________
2. one thousand cycles per second ____________
3. one million cycles per second ____________
4. one billion cycles per second ____________
5. wavelengths in the SHF and EHF bands are called ____________
6. a basic radio wave that carries no information is called a ____________
7. when information is added, the radio wave is said to be ____________
8. adjacent frequencies above and below the carrier frequency ____________
9. determines the information capacity of a channel ____________

C. *Transmitting the signal*

1. the traveling of signals outward from the antenna ____________
2. a station's pattern of signal coverage ____________

3. radio waves in the VHF band that follow a straight path from the transmitting antenna to the horizon ____________________

4. radio waves in the MF band that follow the curvature of the earth ____________________

5. radio waves in the MF and HF bands that are refracted by the ionosphere and achieve great distance ____________________

6. transmission method used in the United States that causes radio waves to oscillate back and forth *across* their propagation path ____________________

7. transmission method that gives receivers a better picture by eliminating ghosts

____

8. transmission method that reinforces radiations in some directions and blocks them in others ____________________

9. the increase in effective radiated power accomplished when radiant energy is concentrated in a particular pattern ____________________

10. the method used to transmit two or more independent signals on the same channel

____

11. a method that uses fewer frequencies by not transmitting redundant information

____

D. *Other terms from the chapter*

1. In sound waves, the frequency determines the ____________________ and the amplitude determines the ____________________.

2. ____________________ account for the qualitative differences between sounds having the same fundamental pitch.

3. AM and FM signal patterns are called ____________________ patterns because their shapes are similar in form to that of the original signal.

4. ______________________ signal processing uses a binary code to break a signal into a stream of separate, individual pulses of energy.

5. The minimum item of information in a binary code is called a ______________________.

6. The process of designating segments of the radio spectrum for specific services is called ______________________.

7. The unused portions of a radio or television channel that are modulated to provide various auxiliary services are called ______________________.

SELF-TEST

Fill in the Blank

1. Radio, visible light, x-rays, and cosmic rays are all forms of ______________________ energy.

2. Sound energy and radio energy have similar wave motion but travel at a different ______________________.

3. An AM radio signal with a frequency of 1500 KHz would have a wavelength of ______________________.

4. While most current broadcast signals consist of analogue patterns, broadcast signals of the future will probably consist of ______________________ patterns.

5. The best location for an FM or TV antenna is ______________________.

6. The signal strength of a transmitting antenna is expressed in terms of its ______________________ rather than in terms of input power.

True/False

T F 1. Frequencies usable for radio communication are located near the lower end of the electromagnetic spectrum.

T **F** 2. Both sound waves and radio waves travel best in an atmosphere of air.

T **F** 3. When two waves of the same frequency are in phase, they cancel each other out.

T **F** 4. When a piano and a violin play the same note, the fundamental pitch is the same but the overtones differ.

T **F** 5. Wavelength can be determined by dividing frequency into velocity.

T **F** 6. When a radio frequency is modulated, sidebands are created.

T **F** 7. Television uses FM for both the video and audio portions of the signal.

T **F** 8. Television uses analogue signal processing for the video portion of the signal and digital processing for the audio portion.

T **F** 9. The transmission range of the television signal can be extended by utilizing sky-wave propagation.

T **F** 10. The broadcast service most dependent on sky-wave propagation is international radio (short wave).

T **F** 11. The higher the frequency of a broadcast channel, the less power it takes to generate a usable signal.

T **F** 12. A television station broadcasting on channel 6 would use a longer transmitting antenna than another station broadcasting on channel 3.

T **F** 13. Directional antennas use phasing to reinforce radiations in one direction and cancel them in another.

T **F** 14. Frequency allocation attempts to match the needs of specific services to the propagation characteristics of specific frequencies.

T **F** 15. Multiplexing expands bandwidth by using additional frequencies to transmit additional services.

PROJECT

Listen to AM radio at night on a quality receiver with a good antenna. Fine tune the dial and see how many AM signals you can pick up from other cities. Note that the number and distance of the stations may vary from evening to evening depending on atmospheric conditions and subsequent sky-wave activity.

CHAPTER 6

Technology of Traditional Broadcasting

CHAPTER FOCUS

This chapter explains many of the procedures established by the Federal Communications Commission to maximize the number of radio and television stations that can broadcast without creating objectionable interference. The chapter also discusses the physical and electronic principles applicable to television and explains how and why the 525-line, 30 fps, NTSC standard was developed.

CAPSULE

Main points from each section of Chapter 6 are summarized below.

6.1 Gaining Access to the Spectrum

A. The Federal Communications Commission designates specific FM and TV channels for use in specific communities. Prospective broadcasters can check the FCC assignment table for a particular community to determine if a channel is available for use.

B. No assignment table exists for AM radio channels. Prospective broadcasters must make engineering studies to determine if a channel can be activated without causing interference with existing stations.

6.2 Interference

A. When two stations broadcast on the same channel, the two signals may create co-channel interference. Co-channel interference is prevented by geographically separating the stations. TV stations using the same channel are separated by a given number of miles (for channel 2, the figure is 220 miles; for a UHF station it is less). The geographic separation required for AM stations is complicated by nighttime sky-wave propagation and varies.

B. When two stations broadcast on nearby channels, the two signals may create adjacent channel interference. TV stations using adjacent channels require a separation of 60 miles. (Remember that channels 4 and 5 are not really adjacent because other services utilize frequencies between the two. The same is true for channels 6 and 7. See Exhibit 6.4 in the text.)

6.3 AM Stations

A. Each AM channel in the United States occupies a bandwidth of 10 kHz. The full AM band runs from 535 to 1,605 kHz, yielding a total bandwidth of 1,070 kHz or enough room for 107 AM channels.

B. The nominal information capacity of an AM station is only half its bandwidth, or 5 kHz. This means that AM stations cannot reproduce frequencies above 5,000 Hz even though the human ear can sometimes distinguish frequencies up to 15,000 Hz.

C. Of the 107 AM channels, the FCC has classified 60 as clear channels, 41 as regional channels, and 6 as local channels. Relatively few stations are assigned to each clear channel, more are assigned to each regional channel, and even more to each local channel.

D. The FCC divides AM stations into four classes designated I, II, III, and IV. Class I stations have dominant status on clear channels. Class II stations have secondary status on clear channels and must limit their power or use directional antennas to avoid interfering with Class I stations on the same frequency. Class III stations are assigned to regional channels, and Class IV stations are placed on local channels.

E. Power authorization varies from 250 watts for some Class IV stations on local channels to 50,000 watts for Class I stations on clear channels. Most Class II, III, and IV stations are required to reduce their power at night and half of all AM stations (most are Class II) must go off the air altogether.

F. Carrier current stations do not emit a broadcast signal. Instead, they radiate a signal either through the steam pipes or power lines of buildings or from wires strung or buried alongside highways. As long as these signals do not interfere with licensed spectrum users, the carrier current stations need not obtain a license from the FCC.

6.4 FM Stations

A. Each FM channel occupies a bandwidth of 0.2 MHz (200 kHz). The full FM band runs from 88 to 108 MHz, yielding a total bandwidth of 20 MHz (20,000 kHz) or enough room for 100 FM channels.

B. Because FM stations broadcast in the VHF band and radiate direct waves rather than ground waves and sky waves, the coverage pattern is the same during all hours of operation.

C. The FCC divides FM stations into three groups designated A, B, and C. Class A stations have power and antenna height restrictions that limit their signal radius to about 15 miles. Class B and Class C stations have signal radii of 30 and 60 miles, respectively.

D. A limited number of very low-power (10 watt) educational stations operate as Class D stations, but even small stations generally use at least 100 watts.

E. FM stations can reproduce sound frequencies as high as 15,000 Hz and provide the listener with a full range of audible sounds. FM signals blank out interference more effectively than AM. FM is largely static-free and has a much greater dynamic range (the ability to distinguish between loudness and softness) than AM radio.

F. FM's 200-kHz bandwidth provides ample space, both for a stereo subcarrier and for various SCA services.

6.5 Shortwave Stations

A. Because international stations broadcast in the HF band and radiate sky waves, coverage is affected by fluctuations in the ionosphere. Engineers are able to predict these fluctuations and determine which frequencies give the best coverage. Consequently, international stations are assigned more than one channel and schedule frequency changes throughout the day and from season to season.

B. Shortwave transmitting antennas are directional, enabling users to beam signals toward a specific area. The Voice of America operates over 30 shortwave transmitters at several domestic sites. A few privately operated shortwave stations in the United States also exist.

6.6 Pictures in Motion

A. Most photographic systems use many tiny picture elements (pixels) to reproduce an image. The size and distribution of these pixels determines the resolution or fineness of detail in the reproduction.

B. In cinema, what appears to be motion is actually a sequence of still pictures or frames. Motion picture photography uses 24 frames-per-second to create the perception of continuity of motion.

C. Each frame is projected twice to overcome flicker. The screen is illuminated 48 times-per-second, and this rapid sequence of images creates the perception of continuity of illumination.

6.7 Electronic Pictures

A. The pickup or picture tube in the television camera breaks each image into thousands of pixels. These bits of light energy are converted into a stream of electrical impulses. Magnetic deflection coils force the electron stream into a systematic or scanning motion. This scanning motion reproduces the image as so many lines of information.

B. Each complete sequence of lines creates a frame. American television engineers developed a system that produces 30 frames-per-second. This figure, rather than the 24 frames-per-second used in motion pictures, was chosen to take advantage of the precise time standard available in 60-hertz alternating current (the standard power available in the United States).

C. Every television frame consists of two fields. One field contains the odd-numbered lines; the alternate field contains the even-numbered lines.

D. The U.S. television standard achieves continuity of motion by electronically creating 30 frames-per-second. Continuity of illumination is achieved by creating 60 fields-per-second, two fields for each frame (Exhibits 6.1 and 6.2).

6.8 The TV Signal

A. The number of lines in each frame determines the vertical resolution of the television image. The United States standard has 525 lines.

B. When the electron beam completes a line, a horizontal blanking interval cuts off the picture pickup during the beam's retrace path. At the completion of a frame, a vertical blanking interval cuts off the picture pickup while the electron beam repositions itself from lower right to upper left to begin scanning the next frame.

C. Sync pulses are created to synchronize camera scanning with that in the receiver.

D. Picture information occupies two thirds of the 6-MHz television channel. Sound information is transmitted on the upper portion of the channel.

E. Color information is added to complete the signal. The color information consists of both hue and luminance. A monochrome receiver uses only the luminance portion of the signal. The American NTSC color standard was the first to resolve the problem of color compatibility and insure that both color and black-and-white receivers could receive the same television signal. Later, improved color systems (PAL and SECAM) were developed in Europe.

6.9 The TV Channel

A. Two-thirds of the 6 MHz in the TV channel is allotted to picture information. The remaining 2 MHz is occupied by the vestigial sideband, the audio channel, and guardbands (Exhibits 6.3 and 6.4).

B. The television resolution achieved with the 525-line, 30-fps American standard is relatively low by modern standards, but higher resolution would require more bandwidth.

6.10 TV Transmission and Reception

A. Audio and video signals are modulated separately, then fed to a diplexer that combines them into a composite signal that goes to the transmitting antenna. TV transmission antennas vary in size according to the wavelength of the channel.

B. Receiving antennas are multichannel and pick up all channels in the VHF or UHF bands. Receiving antennas are highly directional and must be pointed to the signal source. A rotatable outdoor antenna may be necessary if signals come from more than one direction and are more than 20 miles away (Exhibit 6.5).

6.11 Technical Innovations

A. The changeover from vacuum tubes to transistors has enabled engineers to make television equipment much more compact than in the past (Exhibit 6.6).

B. Miniaturization, and specifically the development of the time-base corrector, has given TV stations the ability to provide live news coverage (electronic news gathering or ENG) from nonstudio locations (Exhibit 6.7).

C. High Definition Television (HDTV) is currently in development. This 1,125-line system with a 5 × 3 screen-aspect ratio (instead of the current 4 × 3 screen-aspect ratio) greatly increases the resolution of the television picture, but also requires a bandwidth much greater than the 6 MHz now allotted to TV channels.

D. Because no picture information is transmitted during the vertical blanking interval, additional signals may be multiplexed into the existing 6-MHz channel. One such signal is closed captioning for the hearing impaired. A second is teletext.

KEY TERMS

A. *Terms relating to the assignment of radio or television channels*

1. When two stations are assigned to the same channel, geographic spacing is necessary to

avoid ______________________________ .

2. TV stations assigned to channels 2 and 3 must be at least 60 miles apart to avoid

    ______________________________.

3. Prospective broadcasters can determine the availability of FM or TV channels in a particular community by checking the ______________________________.

4. The FCC has established three categories of channels in the AM band. A limited number of high-power stations are assigned to each of the 60 ______________________________ channels. A greater number of moderate-power stations are assigned to each of the 41 ______________________________ channels, and many low-power stations are assigned to each of the 6 ______________________________ channels.

5. Secondary stations assigned to any of the 60 channels in the first category (see above) are designated ______________________________.

6. Other stations assigned to each of the three types of channels in question 4 are designated ______________________________, ______________________________, and ______________________________ respectively.

7. Very-low-power (10 watt) educational FM stations are designated ____________________.

    Other FM stations are designated ______________________________, ______________________________, and ______________________________ respectively.

8. Low-power AM stations that use steam pipes or power lines rather than the airways to radiate a signal are called ______________________________.

9. A special category of service called ______________________________ uses radiations from wires strung or buried alongside highways. This service is usually found at the bottom (530 kHz) or top (1610 kHz) of the AM dial.

10. There are ______________________________ channels available for assignment in the AM band and each of these channels has a bandwidth of ______________________________.

11. There are ______________________ channels in the FM band and each of these channels has a bandwidth of ______________________.

12. The bandwidth of each television channel is ______________________. This means that ______________________ AM channels could be placed in the spectrum space occupied by one TV channel.

B. *Some miscellaneous terms*

1. Used to describe an FM station's ability to distinguish between very loud and very soft sound ______________________

2. Those services transmitted by FM stations that cannot be detected by ordinary home receivers ______________________

3. The principal American user of international short wave ______________________

4. A New Orleans-based commercial station that transmits on the shortwave band ______________________

C. *Terms relating to television*

1. Most photographic systems break a visual image into many tiny ______________________.

2. The ability of a picture system to provide detail is called its ______________________.

3. Tendency of the eye to retain an image ______________________

4. Problem created when the number of illuminations per second is too low ______________________

5. Visual information is focused on the ______________________ within the TV camera picture tube.

6. The electron stream moves in a systematic or ______________________ motion to read the picture information from the camera tube.

7. This motion is controlled by magnetic fields generated by ______________ that surround the body of the tube.

8. In the American television standard, continuity of motion is achieved by creating a ______________ frequency of ______________ whereas continuity of illumination requires a ______________ frequency of ______________.

9. The process of combining the two halves of a television picture is called ______________.

10. The number of lines in a TV picture determines its ______________.

11. Breaks in the scanning of the electron beam are called ______________.

12. Signals that keep scanning in the camera at a television studio in step with scanning in the picture tubes of the home receivers are called ______________.

13. Color information consists of ______________ and ______________.

14. The ability of monochrome receivers to interpret color pictures as black-and-white images is called ______________.

15. The color television standard used in the American system is called ______________. Two standards used in Europe are called ______________ and ______________.

16. There are ______________ lines of information in the American system. The British and European countries use a different system with ______________ lines.

17. Some facsimile systems deliver still pictures over an extended period. Television, however, delivers all the information needed for moving pictures in ______________.

18. The pulses that drive the camera's deflection coils and control scanning come from a

_______________.

19. The cathode-ray tube or picture tube in the television receiver is called a

_______________.

20. The reduction in size and weight of television equipment would not have been possible without the invention of _______________.

21. Electronic news gathering (ENG) would not have been possible without the development of the _______________.

22. Information for closed captioning and teletext can be multiplexed in the _______________ of the television signal.

SELF-TEST

Fill in the Blank

1. The information capacity of any radio channel is determined by its _______________.

2. Nighttime interference is a much greater problem for _______________ than for _______________ and _______________.

3. Class I stations have dominant status on _______________ channels.

4. The maximum allowable power for AM stations in the United States is

_______________.

5. Shortwave transmission is used by the U.S. government's official external service, the

_______________.

6. The perception of moving pictures, whether on film or with television, requires both continuity of _______________ and continuity of _______________.

7. The NTSC color system was adopted, in part, because it provided ______________________ with existing monochrome receivers.

8. Smaller and lighter TV equipment has enabled news crews to leave the confines of the studio and travel to the location of a story. This newer portable technique is called

______________________________.

True/False

T F 1. FM channels are assigned from an FCC table, but AM channels are assigned on a station-by-station or ad hoc basis.

T F 2. In audio, full fidelity requires a bandwidth of 15,000 hertz.

T F 3. The nominal information capacity of an AM channel is 5 kHz.

T F 4. Only a Class I station may broadcast on a clear channel.

T F 5. There are 100 channels in the AM band and 107 channels in the FM band.

T F 6. FM radio gives a better sound than AM radio because it has three distinct advantages—greater frequency response, dynamic range, and freedom from static.

T F 7. A listener to shortwave radio may find it necessary to re-tune his or her receiver because international stations change frequencies at various times of the day.

T F 8. The American television standard creates an image with approximately the same resolution or detail as that found in 35-mm motion pictures.

T F 9. The television image is really just a rapid sequence of pixels.

T F 10. American TV has a higher vertical resolution than British television.

T F 11. The 12 frequencies used for TV in the United States are actually found in three different portions of the VHF band.

T F 12. UHF stations are permitted to broadcast at a much higher power than VHF stations because UHF waves attenuate more rapidly than VHF waves.

T F 13. The term *solid state* refers specifically to the silicon chips now used in microcomputers and soon to be applied to television technology.

T F 14. Electronic news gathering would not have been possible without the development of the time-base corrector.

T F 15. Closed captioning is placed on the audio subcarrier of the composite television signal.

PROJECT

Are there any TV or FM channels allotted to your community that are not in use? Check the FCC assignment table in *Broadcasting-Cable Yearbook.* Also determine the type of each AM station in your community. How is each station classified? For how much power is each station licensed, and what, if any, requirements are imposed on hours of operation and the use of directional antennas?

CHAPTER 7

Delivery, Distribution, and Storage

CHAPTER FOCUS

This chapter deals with technical aspects of syndication. Chapters 8-9 deal with economic aspects. Most television programs and many radio programs are not aired "live." They are produced and stored on video- and audiotape and distributed by broadcast and cable networks to affiliate stations or cable systems. Most of this distribution is now done by satellite relay.

CAPSULE

Main points from each section of Chapter 7 are summarized below.

7.1 Basic Concepts

A. Program producers may be considered as wholesalers who distribute their products to local stations (the retailers) who, in turn, deliver those products to end-users (the viewers and listeners). The entire process is called *syndication.*

B. News agencies, motion picture and music distributors, and broadcast networks are all forms of syndication.

C. A network is simply two or more stations connected in a way that allows each station to broadcast simultaneously identical programs to more than one market. Networks require relay links that pass the signal from one station to another. Initially, these links consisted of telephone lines. Later, microwave relays and satellite technology provided the interconnections.

D. The potential for syndication revenue is even greater if program materials can be stored for reuse. Various methods of recording are available, including film and magnetic tape.

E. Most of the programs broadcast today are prerecorded. Only news, sports, and special events are broadcast live.

7.2 Sound Recording

A. Audio discs were the first recorded materials. Most discs use a stylus (commonly called a needle) that vibrates in concentric analogue grooves. Newer technology uses a laser beam that tracks digitally processed sound (Exhibit 7.1).

B. Magnetic tape eliminated some of the mechanical operation inherent in older discs and greatly improved portability and convenience. Originally, all tape recorders used reel-to-reel configuration. Later, cartridge and cassette tape recorders, with their greater convenience, took over both broadcast and consumer markets.

7.3 Picture Recording

A. Initially, specially designed motion picture cameras photographed the images from a television monitor. These *kinescope recordings* were of poor quality and, after the invention of magnetic recording, were unsuitable for broadcast use.

B. Magnetic recording techniques, already developed for audio, were applied to television. But visual images contain hundreds of times more information than does sound. A tape speed of $7\frac{1}{2}$ inches per second (ips) produced a satisfactory audio recording, but an effective speed of 1,500 ips was necessary to record pictures.

C. Ampex engineers achieved this very high speed by using a revolving drum with four magnetic heads that moved transversely across the 2-inch tape while the tape moved longitudinally from supply to pick-up reel. These first videotape machines were called *quadruplex* recorders.

D. Subsequently, less expensive machines were developed that used 1-inch and smaller tape stock and a less complicated magnetic head configuration. These machines were called *helical* recorders because the tape moved in a spiral or helical pattern and the magnetic head or heads created a slanted track as they placed the video information on the tape (Exhibit 7.2).

E. In some helical machines, the tape is enclosed in a cassette rather than in the more traditional reel-to-reel format. These videocassette recorders have become extremely popular because of their portability and ease of operation. The three-quarter-inch U-matic format is used by many broadcasters but two half-inch formats—Betamax and VHS—are also in use. Other formats have been developed that use 8 mm and even quarter-inch tape.

7.4 Terrestrial Relays

A. For many years, land-based (terrestrial) relay circuits provided the network interconnection with affiliate stations.

B. Ordinary telephone circuits could be used for radio. Coaxial cable (Exhibit 7.3) was necessary to transmit the greater bandwidths needed for television.

C. Microwave relay techniques replaced coaxial cable as the principal means of transmitting television signals. Microwave networks do not require a right-of-way and are easier to maintain, particularly in rugged terrain.

D. The newest terrestrial relay techniques use optical fiber conductors. These fiber-optic strands have the ability to transmit bandwidths in the thousands of megahertz.

7.5 Space Relays

A. Communication satellites can be compared to microwave relay towers 22,300 miles tall. Satellites, unlike relay towers, can transmit signals to an unlimited number of receiving earth stations. Signal attenuation is also less of a problem because each signal passes through a relatively few miles of atmosphere on its way to and from the satellite.

B. Satellites perform their relay functions best when they remain in a fixed position relative to the earth. These satellites are said to be in a geosynchronous orbit (Exhibit 7.4).

C. Certain superhigh frequencies have been allocated for broadcast satellite use. The C band uses 4 to 6 gigahertz; the Ku band uses 11 to 15 gigahertz. Each band is wide enough to accommodate many different channels for simultaneous transmissions. Half of these channels are used to uplink signals from transmitting earth stations to the satellite's transponders; the other half are used to downlink signals from the transponders to receiving earth stations.

D. Transponders can downlink or transmit to a broad *footprint* covering almost a third of the earth's surface or they can downlink a directional *spot-beam* covering a relatively small area.

7.6 Over-the-Air Hybrids

A. *Rebroadcasting* combines delivery and relay functions into a single operation. Most rebroadcasting in the United States utilizes *translators.* These unattended repeater stations receive a signal on one frequency and retransmit it on a different frequency to avoid-co-channel interference.

B. *Instructional Television Fixed Service (ITFS)* uses 20 microwave channels at the high end of the UHF band to transmit TV signals up to 25 miles. These channels are used primarily by schools and universities.

C. *Multipoint Distribution Service (MDS)* operates as a common carrier. It leases individual channels in the ITFS frequencies and serves as a link between program suppliers and pay TV customers. *Multichannel Multipoint Distribution Service (MMDS)* allows the operator to use four channels in the ITFS band and provide consumers with greater program choice.

D. *Teletext* uses television broadcasting to deliver printed material. One use for teletext is captions for the hearing-impaired. Full pages of information can either be superimposed over a television picture or viewed independently. The number of pages that can be transmitted in the vertical blanking interval of a television signal is limited to around 300.

E. *Direct-broadcast satellite (DBS)* combines relay and delivery functions by transmitting a signal from the program source directly to consumers. DBS operates in the Ku band. It must deliver a relatively high-powered signal because individual receiving antennas are only 2 to 3 feet in diameter.

7.7 Cable Television

A. Cable television, initially known as Community Antenna Television or CATV, delivers both broadcast and nonbroadcast materials to subscribers' homes. Numerous signals are either received at or originate from the *headend.* These signals are then delivered through heavy *trunk cables* to smaller *feeder cables* and eventually to *drop cables* that bring the signals to individual homes (Exhibit 7.6).

B. Cable operators can deliver as many as 60 channels by placing signals on channels 2 through 13 and also on other VHF frequencies not available for over-the-air transmission (Exhibit 7.7).

7.8 Special Cable Features

A. One or more channels can be designated for *pay cable.* Pay cable provides special nonbroadcast programming to customers who pay extra for the service. Either frequency-blocking electronic traps or signal-scrambling technology (usually the latter) is used to prevent nonpay subscribers from receiving these channels.

B. *Interactive cable* permits subscribers to select service on a pay-per-program as well as a pay-per-channel basis. Customers use an addressable converter to send orders upstream to the cable headend. The headend then addresses information to the subscriber's converter that allows the signal to be processed.

C. *Master antenna television (MTV)* is a mini-cable system confined to a single building or a group of adjacent buildings.

D. *Videotex* provides printed material similar in appearance to that supplied by teletext, but the method of transmission is very different. Videotex is transmitted by telephone lines or by cable rather than broadcast as a portion of a television signal. Videotex is two-way; subscribers call up desired pages and the system responds accordingly. Because videotex has its own full channel, the number of pages is far greater–often a thousand or more.

E. Cable systems will frequently set aside one or more channels to display news, weather, program listings, or other printed information. The display may be static or changing. This service is called *cabletext.*

KEY TERMS

A. *Terms relating to the distribution of radio and TV programs*

1. Many programs are centrally produced and widely distributed to a number of stations who each pay a portion of the cost. These programs are said to be in ____________________.

2. When two or more stations interconnect to broadcast the same material to different markets, they have formed a ____________________.

3. Each of the interconnecting elements is called a ____________________.

4. The interconnection is not provided by the stations themselves but rather by specialized firms called ____________________ who provide such service to all comers for a fixed, government-regulated rate.

5. Although telephone lines can be used to interconnect radio stations, television's greater bandwidth requires a special ____________________ cable.

6. Because these cables are difficult to lay in mountainous terrain, most interconnection is now accomplished by ____________________.

7. The newest form of cable, called ______________________, uses an extremely pure glass to transmit bandwidth in the thousands of megahertz.

8. When a satellite is in a fixed position relative to the earth, it is said to be in a

   ______________________ orbit.

9. Satellite positions are designated in degrees of longitude east or west of the

   ______________________.

10. Satellites use two bands of frequencies. One in the 4 to 6 gigahertz region is known as the

    ______________________ band; the second in the 11 to 15 gigahertz region is

    designated as the ______________________ band.

11. Any satellite distribution requires two distinct transmissions—one from the originating point to the satellite, the second from the satellite to receivers. The first is called an

    ______________________, the second a ______________________.

12. The vital element in each satellite that receives and retransmits signals is called a

    ______________________.

13. The satellite's ______________________ is that portion of the earth's surface covered by the retransmitted signal.

14. The retransmitted signal is very weak and must first pass through a

    ______________________. Then it goes to a ______________________ that changes the superhigh frequencies into lower frequencies more usable for TV receivers.

B. *Terms relating to the storage of radio and TV programs*

1. Phonographs use a ______________________ that vibrates as it mechanically tracks analogue information contained in the grooves of a record during playback.

2. The newer CD or ______________________ format uses a

   ______________________ to pick up digital information from the record surface.

3. Originally, all magnetic tape recorders had open feed and take-up reels. Later, many recorders enclosed both reels into a single unit called a ____________________.

4. Other recorders use a single hub and an endless tape loop that permits repetitive playback of the same material. These ____________________ machines are widely used in radio stations.

5. TV's first recording technique used a motion picture camera to photograph the picture tube. The resulting films were known as ____________________.

6. The first videotape recorders were called ____________________ machines because they used four recording heads to create a ____________________ track of information across the width of the tape.

7. Later videotape recorders used one or two heads to create an angular or ____________________-track of information. These recorders are often called ____________________ because of the path followed by the magnetic tape.

8. Portable videotape recorders that use three-quarter inch tape are called ____________________.

9. Other videotape recorders use one-half inch tape. The two leading formats are called ____________________ and ____________________.

C. *Terms relating to the delivery of radio and TV programs*

1. Unattended repeater stations called ____________________ pick up broadcast signals and rebroadcast them on another frequency to otherwise uncovered areas.

2. Programming may be originated by a special category of secondary-status television stations called ____________________.

3. A special band of microwave channels created by the FCC for use by educational institutions is called ____________________.

4. When one of these microwave channels is used by a commercial carrier to deliver programs to home TV receivers, it is called ______________________________.

5. An expanded version of the above service called ______________________________ delivers four channels rather than one to subscribers.

6. ______________________________ is a hybrid service that blends elements of television broadcasting and print media by using the vertical blanking interval of the TV signal to transmit textual and graphic material.

7. Satellites that combine relay and delivery functions and transmit TV signals directly to consumers rather than to television stations or cable systems are called ______________________________.

8. Initially, cable television was known as ______________________________.

9. A cable TV firm assembles programs at the system's ______________________________ for transmission to subscriber homes.

10. The special microwave relay used by cable systems to pick up distant TV stations is called ______________________________.

11. Cable systems use a tree-and-branch pattern to distribute signals to subscriber homes. The heaviest ______________________________ cables branch to lighter ______________________________ cables and then to still lighter ______________________________ cables.

12. Cable provides basic service to all subscribers and additional ______________________________ services to those subscribers willing to pay extra fees.

13. Systems that allow a subscriber to send messages upstream to the cable office are said to be ______________________________.

14. Private cable systems confined to a single building complex are called ______________________________.

15. A two-way text-and-graphics medium that uses either cable or telephone lines to interconnect the user with the data base is called ________________.

16. One-way, full-channel text services used by cable systems to display news, weather, and other kinds of information are called ________________.

SELF-TEST

Fill in the Blank

1. Syndication of radio and television programs involves three basic functions—delivery, distribution, and storage. Broadcast stations and cable systems are most closely identified with the ________________ function while networks perform the ________________ function.

2. Even before broadcasting was possible, technology enabled the storage of musical performances on ________________.

3. Portability and convenience in sound recording was greatly improved with the development of ________________.

4. Broadcast-quality picture storage was not possible until the development of the ________________ in 1956.

5. Earthbound systems that provide the interconnection for network broadcasting are called ________________ relays.

6. Satellite systems provide a similar function in space. Although the signal travels a much greater distance, ________________ is less of a problem because the signal is reamplified only once.

7. Most U.S. and foreign satellites are launched by ________________, although a competitive launch facility is located in French Guiana.

8. The term *wireless cable* is sometimes applied to ________________.

9. Cable systems transmit all signals in the ________________ frequency band because attenuation is too great a problem in the ________________ band.

10. An interactive cable system enables subscribers to send messages ________________ to the cable headend.

True/False

T **F** 1. The first syndicators were Associated Press, Reuters, and other news agencies.

T **F** 2. Broadcast stations and networks are classified as common carriers.

T **F** 3. Standard phonograph records use digital signal processing, but CDs use analogue signal processing.

T **F** 4. Audiocassettes use an endless reel of tape and are widely used in automated radio stations.

T **F** 5. Videotape recorders combine head-and-tape movement to achieve the writing speed necessary to process the large amount of information in a television signal.

T **F** 6. Betamax and VHS videocassette recorders are compatible.

T **F** 7. Both radio and television signals can be distributed with ordinary telephone circuits.

T **F** 8. Optical fiber cables can transmit a much greater bandwidth than coaxial cables.

T **F** 9. Degradation of signal quality is a greater problem in satellite relays than in terrestrial relays because the signal travels a much greater distance.

T **F** 10. Geosynchronous satellites are positioned 22,300 miles above the earth's equator.

T **F** 11. Satellites can deliver a signal in either a broad footprint or a directional spot-beam.

T **F** 12. Many of the television translators currently in use are located in the sparsely settled, mountainous areas of the country.

T **F** 13. Videotex is a one-way system that uses a portion of the television signal, whereas teletext is a two-way wired system.

T **F** 14. Cable makes use of VHF frequencies not available for over-the-air television transmission.

T **F** 15. Pay cable requires addressable converters and interactive systems.

PROJECT

Locate a copy of *Satellite News* or a similar publication in your library. How many satellites are currently in orbit? Note the longitudinal placement of various satellites. Also note the number of transponders on each satellite and the usage made of each transponder.

PART 3

Economics

CHAPTER 8

Stations, Systems, and Networks

CHAPTER FOCUS

This chapter discusses the organization and structure of commercial and noncommercial broadcast stations and cable systems. It also examines the contractual relationship between broadcast networks and their affiliate stations and between cable networks and the systems that carry their programming. Employment opportunities in broadcasting, cable, and related industries are explored.

CAPSULE

Main points from each section of Chapter 8 are summarized below.

8.1 The Commercial Broadcast Station

A. The organizational structure of commercial radio and television stations reflects the four functions these stations perform. The functions are classified as general/administrative, technical, programming, and sales (Exhibit 8.1).

B. Stations may be owned individually or in groups. Many stations, particularly those in larger markets, are group-owned. Some of the better-known group owners include Cox, Metromedia, Taft, and Westinghouse.

C. *O & O* stations are group stations owned and operated by ABC, CBS, and NBC. These stations are located in New York, Los Angeles, Chicago, and other major markets. Each network's group of O & O stations reaches more than 20 percent of the nation's television households.

8.2 Commercial Broadcast Networks and Affiliates

A. Networks that distribute programs during a substantial part of each day to all parts of the United States are described as *full-service*. Other networks created for parttime or occasional distribution are called *ad hoc* networks (Exhibit 8.2).

B. About three-fourths of the commercial TV stations are classified as network *affiliates.* Each affiliate has a contractual relationship with ABC, CBS, or NBC that gives that station the first option to air network programs in its markets. If an affiliate chooses not to air a network program, however, that program can be offered to another station.

C. Broadcast affiliates do not pay to air network programs. Rather, networks pay the affiliates to carry the programs and their accompanying commercials. This *network compensation* to affiliates is based on the hypothetical value of each station's time and varies widely according to such factors as market size and station popularity.

D. About one-fourth of the commercial TV stations have no affiliation with ABC, CBS, or NBC. These stations are classified as *independents* and must produce or purchase all of the programming they air. As a group, independents lost money until 1975, but improved programming has brought larger viewing audiences and profits have responded accordingly.

E. Contracts between affiliates and networks are renewable every two years. Affiliates may refuse to grant clearance time for network programs or even preempt time already cleared in order to substitute programming from another source. Low-rated network public-affairs programs are frequently delayed or preempted altogether by affiliates who substitute movies or other profitable entertainment-oriented programs. Networks can and sometimes do refuse to renew affiliation contracts with stations that repeatedly preempt network offerings.

8.3 Noncommercial Broadcasting

A. Noncommercial stations perform the same four functions as commercial stations, but the term *development* is substituted for sales. Development encompasses the many fund-raising activities of each station.

B. Public television stations are also categorized according to ownership. The largest number of stations are owned by state or municipal agencies. The most influential are community stations owned by nonprofit corporations in larger metropolitan areas. These community stations produce most of the programs aired by PBS. University and school stations are the two remaining categories.

C. Public radio stations are categorized by their affiliation or nonaffiliation with National Public Radio (Exhibit 8.3). Larger stations qualify for funding from the Corporation for Public Broadcasting and affiliation with NPR; smaller stations do not.

D. The Corporation for Public Broadcasting (CPB) is a quasi-governmental agency created to encourage and support noncommercial broadcasting. It receives most of its money from the federal budget via Congressional appropriations and transmits that money to stations, networks, and producing agencies.

E. The Public Broadcasting Service (PBS) maintains the satellite interconnection that distributes TV programs to affiliate stations. PBS does not produce programs but acts as a clearinghouse for programs produced by member stations and selected for funding through the Station Program Cooperative.

F. National Public Radio (NPR) produces programs and maintains the satellite interconnection that distributes its own and other radio programs to affiliate stations.

8.4 Cable Systems and Networks

A. Cable systems also perform the same four functions as commercial stations. However, the programming function involves many different channels. Some programming comes from over-the-air television stations, some from local origination and access channels, and some from cable networks.

B. The sales function is twofold—it involves the sale of advertising spots on certain channels but, more importantly, it involves the marketing of various services to current and potential subscribers.

C. Most cable systems are operated by Multiple System Operators or MSOs. These are the cable equivalent of group owners in broadcasting. Some of the major MSOs are Cox, Storer, Viacom, and Times Mirror (Exhibit 8.4).

D. Cable systems retransmit the signals of local television stations. They also carry three additional categories of program service. These include advertiser-supported networks such as the Cable News Network (CNN) and the Entertainment and Sports Network (ESPN), premium networks such as Home Box Office (HBO) and Showtime, and superstations such as WTBS, WGN, and WOR (Exhibits 8.5 and 8.6).

8.5 Employment

A. The total number of people working in broadcasting and cable is relatively small—only about 300,000 fulltime employees (Exhibit 8.7).

B. Broadcast and cable operations with five or more employees are required to file an Equal Employment Opportunities report with the FCC. Consequently, there is a subtle pressure to increase the percentage of women and minorities employed in positions of importance (see Box in text).

C. Unionization in broadcasting and cable is substantial, particularly in larger markets. Unions generally fall into two categories—those associated with performance or talent such as AFTRA or SAG, and those involved with technical functions such as IBEW, NABET, and IATSE.

D. The fewest jobs for newcomers to broadcasting and cable are in performance and production; the greatest job opportunities are in news, promotion, and sales. Many individuals with broadcast-related skills will find employment in the growing *industrial-video* field (see Box in text).

KEY TERMS

A. *Terms relating to commercial broadcast stations and networks*

1. The placement of commercial, promotional, and public service announcements within and between programs is the responsibility of the ____________________ department.

2. This department prepares a daily ____________________ that provides a minute-by-minute schedule of all program items and announcements.

3. When technical or other reasons prevent a commercial announcement from being aired as scheduled, the station must provide a ____________________.

4. Commercial openings not yet sold to advertisers are referred to as

______________________________.

5. Cox, Metromedia, Taft, and Westinghouse are among the best known of the non-network

______________________________.

6. Broadcast stations owned by ABC, CBS, or NBC are called ______________________________ stations.

7. A national organization that distributes programs for a substantial part of each day to

stations in all parts of the United States is called a ______________________________ network.

8. WXXX is interconnected with and provides live coverage of football games for seven

other stations. This would be an example of an ______________________________ network.

9. Stations that carry most programming provided by any particular network are

______________________________ of that network.

10. When a station carries programming from two or more networks, it is said to be a

______________________________ of the lessor network(s).

11. Stations with no network affiliation are called ______________________________.

12. The ______________________________ forbids television affiliates in the fifty largest markets from accepting more than three hours of network programming during the prime-time period.

13. The ______________________________ between a network and each of its affiliate stations is renewable every two years and may be allowed to lapse by either party at expiration.

14. Stations receive a payment called ______________________________ for airing network programs.

15. FCC rules prohibit network contracts from containing ______________________________ rules that prevent affiliates from accepting non-network programs or networks from placing programs with other stations.

16. Affiliate stations grant ______________________________ for most network programming.

17. When stations substitute their own programs for network programs, they are said to ______________________________ the network programs.

B. *Terms relating to noncommercial broadcasting*

1. The Public Broadcasting Act of 1967, an amendment to the Communications Act of 1934, created the ______________________________ to facilitate the development of educational noncommercial broadcasting.

2. Interconnection of noncommercial television stations is provided by the ______________________________.

3. Interconnection of noncommercial radio stations as well as the production of some programs is provided by ______________________________.

4. Those public radio stations that meet certain minimum standards in terms of power, programming facilities, number of fulltime employees, and total operating budget are said to be ______________________________.

5. Public television stations jointly select and agree to fund programs through a mechanism known as the ______________________________.

C. *Terms relating to cable systems and networks*

1. The number of subscribers to any cable service is continually changing. This subscriber turnover is known as ______________________________.

2. Some cable systems are interconnected by cable or microwave. Other systems exchange video tapes. The first group maintains a ______________________________ interconnect; the second a ______________________________ interconnect.

3. While many early cable systems were "Mom and Pop" operations, current ownership trends are putting many cable systems in the hands of ______________________________ .

4. The FCC ______________________________ rule used to require each cable system to retransmit the signals of all television stations operating within 35 miles of the community served by that system.

5. TV stations such as WTBS and WOR whose signals are distributed by satellite to cable systems throughout the country are called ______________________________.

D. *Terms and organizations relating to employment in broadcasting and cable*

1. The FCC requires broadcast stations and cable systems with five or more employees to submit an annual report classifying employees according to job category, sex, and minority status. This is done to enforce provisions of the ______________________________ Act.

2. The first purely broadcasting union and the one that represents most radio and television performers is the ______________________________.

3. Both film and television script writers are represented by the ______________________________.

4. Actors who appear in films are represented by the ______________________________.

5. This union was the first to negotiate ______________________________ clauses in contracts that require payments to actors for reruns of television programs.

6. In broadcasting, three different unions represent technical workers. Provide the initials of each union: ______________________________, ______________________________, ______________________________.

SELF-TEST

Fill in the Blank

1. All broadcast stations perform four basic functions and organize their staffs accordingly.

These four functions include ______________________,

______________________, ______________________, and

______________________.

2. The three television networks receive over one-third of their revenue from the operation of profitable ______________________ stations in major markets.

3. Despite gains by independents in audience size and profit, which category of station continues to dominate television viewing hours and advertising revenue? ______________________

4. How frequently must affiliation contracts between networks and stations be renewed?

____

5. Who selects the programs distributed by PBS and aired by noncommercial television stations?

____

6. Although cable companies do sell commercial time on certain channels, most of their revenue comes from ______________________.

7. HBO and Showtime are examples of ______________________ cable networks.

8. Under EEO rules, stations and cable systems are required to report the employment status of ______________________ and ______________________.

9. Most technical jobs in major market television stations require ______________________ membership.

10. The best employment opportunities for newcomers to the broadcasting industry are in

______________________.

True/False

T F 1. Although news is a part of programming, most radio and television stations treat it as a separate department.

T F 2. Cox, Metromedia, Taft, ABC, CBS, and NBC all qualify as group owners of broadcast stations.

T F 3. *Evening* and *PM Magazine* were created to fill time made available by the prime-time access rule.

T F 4. Each of the three television networks has around two hundred affiliates.

T F 5. Both networks and affiliates benefited from the introduction of the prime-time access rule.

T F 6. ABC, NBC, and CBS receive a network compensation from affiliate stations who pay to air the programs the networks provide.

T F 7. Affiliate stations have the right to preempt network programming and substitute their own programming at any time in the broadcast schedule.

T F 8. The most influential noncommercial television stations and the ones that produce much of the programming seen on PBS are under state or municipal control.

T F 9. All noncommercial radio stations receive programming from NPR.

T F 10. Cable systems are required to function independently and may not interconnect to share program materials.

T F 11. Cable systems must pay fees to carry both advertiser-supported networks such as CNN and superstations such as WTBS.

T F 12. Approximately 3 million fulltime employees work in broadcasting and cable.

T F 13. Residuals are of greatest concern to members of the NABET, IBEW, and IATSE.

T F 14. Industrial video is a growing field that offers employment opportunities in the nonbroadcast uses of television.

T F 15. Historically, the highest managerial positions in broadcasting and cable have been filled from the ranks of sales personnel.

PROJECT

Broadcasting Yearbook contains a listing of key executives for every broadcast station and every network. Examine the listings for the stations in your community. Note the titles and responsibilities of these individuals. Then do the same for the three commercial television networks and for PBS.

CHAPTER 9

Broadcast and Cable Advertising

CHAPTER FOCUS

Commercial broadcasters depend on income from advertising as their sole form of support. Cable systems receive the bulk of their income from subscriber fees but look to advertising as a growing source of revenue. Chapter 9 explains many of the business practices used by broadcasters and cable operators when dealing with advertisers and their agencies.

CAPSULE

Main points from each section of Chapter 9 are summarized below.

9.1 Advantages of Broadcast Advertising

A. Radio and TV advertising can reach consumers both inside and outside the home and during the times when they are most susceptible to the mention of certain products. TV has the unique combination of sight, sound, movement, and color that allows advertisers to demonstrate their products to potential buyers.

B. Well-produced commercials can be entertaining and thus hold the attention of viewers and listeners. TV's status as a trusted medium is frequently transferred to the products it advertises.

C. Broadcast advertising may be local, network, or national spot (Exhibits 9.1 and 9.2). The first category involves local advertisers who purchase time on local stations. The second involves national advertisers who buy commercial time on network programs carried by affiliate stations. The third, national spot advertising, is purchased by national and regional advertisers who buy time in various markets on a station-by-station basis.

D. Cooperative (co-op) advertising is a hybrid of local and national spot advertising. A local retailer purchases the ad and shares the cost with the national distributor whose product is featured in the commercial.

E. Time may be purchased for program sponsorship or on a participatory advertising basis. Traditional sponsorship, now rare, involves the purchase of a block of time and gives the advertiser control of program content as well as the right to utilize all commercial spots within that program. In participatory advertising, the advertiser along with other advertisers buys one or more spots and thereby participates in the sponsorship of a program. The true sponsor, at least from the standpoint of determining program content, is the network or station.

9.2 Disadvantages of Broadcast Advertising

A. The boundaries of broadcast advertising are determined by the coverage of a station's signal rather than the particular needs of the advertiser. Smaller businesses find broadcast advertising wasteful and prefer cable, direct mail, suburban newspapers, and other localized media to reach their target audiences more efficiently.

B. Broadcast advertising is sometimes expensive and always transitory. Remote-control tuning devices allow viewers to avoid commercials by switching to another channel. The fast-forward function on videocassette recorders allows viewers to bypass or "zap" commercials when they play back a program.

C. Time limitations constrain the amount of information that can be presented in the usual 20- or 30-second commercial. Standards of taste restrict presentation techniques and even forbid the advertising of certain products.

D. The trend to shorter commercials has brought with it a tendency to air more commercials in a particular time slot. This *clutter* undermines the effectiveness of the individual messages.

9.3 Broadcast Commercials and Announcements

A. Sponsor identification is required by Section 317 of the Communications Act of 1934. When a station receives payment to air any item of content, it must disclose the source of that payment. This disclosure usually takes the form of a commercial spot; it may include a credit near the end of a program.

B. Commercials are scheduled during natural breaks in program content. Care is usually taken to separate the airing of commercials from other commercials for competing products.

C. Programs that have neither sponsorship nor participatory advertising are called sustaining programs. These nonsupported programs are aired by stations and networks as a public service.

D. Commercials are placed within programs and during the interval between programs (or between portions of longer programs) when stations make identification announcements (IDs). The actual ID takes only a few seconds; the ID interval can usually accommodate several commercial spots.

E. Promos (promotional announcements) and PSAs (public service announcements) resemble commercials and are scheduled by the traffic department into available spots throughout the broadcast day.

9.4 Cable Advertising

A. Advertising on cable accounts for less than 1 percent of all advertising expenditures, but the amount in dollars and in percentage is increasing. Cable shares many of television's advantages and disadvantages, with some variations.

B. Smaller merchants can use cable to reach a localized population. All advertisers can use specialized cable channels to reach audiences with predictable demographic characteristics, for example, ESPN and MTV.
C. Cable allows greater flexibility in the length and content of commercials.
D. Limited audience measurement information is cable's most serious handicap. The elaborate ratings data that Nielsen and Arbitran provide for broadcast stations are not yet available for local cable. Without such data, advertisers are reluctant to commit more than a small fraction of their budget to cable advertising.

9.5 Advertising Rates

A. Market size (Exhibit 9.4), station coverage, and network affiliation are three factors that affect the prices stations charge for commercial time. The principal variable is the size and composition of the audience.
B. The relationship between audience and price is reflected in the cost-per-thousand formulation. (Cost-per-thousand is referred to as CPM; the M being the Roman numeral for 1,000. See Box.) Station salespeople will quote prospective advertisers a CPM for both total audience and for specific demographic groups.
C. The effectiveness of broadcast advertising is dependent on a cumulative effect. Commercial spots are almost never bought singly but rather in groups or packages. The number of spots in the package and the placement of each spot determines the cost of the package.
D. Radio stations typically divide their time into day parts and price their spots accordingly (Exhibit 9.3). Spots during morning drive time when audiences are greatest command the highest prices; late-night spots bring the lowest prices.
E. Rates for television spots are much more variable than for radio. Rates often vary on a program-by-program basis and are subject to negotiation.
F. Run-of-schedule (ROS) spots may be scheduled during various time periods throughout the day and during different times on different days. ROS spots are more common in radio but are available in television.
G. Preemptible spots are sold at a lower rate than fixed spots.
H. Cable rates vary widely but are generally much lower than those for TV stations. Some cable systems are interconnected, giving advertisers the opportunity to purchase time on several systems in the same metropolitan area.
I. Commercial spots are generally sold for cash but some stations will exchange commercial time for goods and service. These noncash transactions are called barters, trade deals, or trade-outs. A few stations will sell spots during marginal time periods on a per-inquiry basis.

9.6 Selling Advertising

A. Salespeople, often called account executives, generally receive the highest pay among radio and television employees. Compensation is usually on a commission basis.
B. Account executives from various stations compete with one another for radio or TV dollars. They also try to persuade advertisers to change their media mix by spending more on radio or TV and less on print (Exhibit 9.5).
C. National sales representation firms (reps) secure national spot advertising for the stations they represent. A typical rep firm may represent one hundred or more stations in as many markets.

D. All national and regional advertisers and most local advertisers use advertising agencies (Exhibit 9.6). These agencies develop campaigns, prepare commercials, and buy time from stations on behalf of their clients. Agencies traditionally receive a 15 percent commission on billings. For example, an agency purchases time valued at $100,000 from station WXXX. The agency collects $100,000 from its client, but pays only $85,000 to the station. The $15,000 balance is the agency's commission.

9.7 Advertising Standards and Practices

A. Time and taste standards are continually evolving. A few years ago commercials for feminine-hygiene products and hemorrhoid preparations were prohibited; now they are commonplace. Commercials for contraceptives are being aired on an experimental basis by some stations during certain time periods.

B. Each station decides the number of minutes in a broadcast hour it wishes to allocate for commercials. For some years, many stations followed voluntary time standards established by the National Association of Broadcasters, but these standards were set aside after the Justice Department claimed they violated antitrust laws.

C. The FCC maintains that the marketplace and not government can best control the amount of commercial time a station airs. Presumably, greedy stations that air too many commercials will lose their audiences and eventually their advertisers.

D. Each of the networks, each group owner, and many individual stations have program and advertising standards that are used to judge the appropriateness of questionable programs or commercials.

E. The Federal Trade Commission (FTC) has the responsibility to insure that advertising is neither fraudulent nor deceptive. The FTC may require an advertiser to provide proof to substantiate an advertising claim.

F. Advertising directed to children is a particularly sensitive issue. Action for Children's Television (ACT), a consumer group, has long advocated regulations to protect children from commercial exploitation. Their most recent concern involves cartoons that feature toys such as *He-Man* and *GI Joe* as principal characters in the programs. These make the cartoons, in ACT's view, nothing more than program-length commercials.

G. FCC and congressional actions have made four kinds of unethical business practices illegal. These include plugola, payola, double billing, and clipping.

KEY TERMS

A. *Types and categories of advertising*

1. A business that purchases time from radio or TV stations in its own communities is an example of ______________________ advertising.

2. National advertisers who purchase time within network programming are an example of ______________________ advertising.

3. National advertisers who buy radio or TV spots on a station-by-station basis are an

   example of ______________________________ advertising.

4. When the content and the cost of a commercial are shared between the national manufacturer of a product and the local distributor, this commercial is classified as

   ______________________________ advertising.

5. When an advertiser purchases a block of time and takes responsibility for all content aired

   during that time period, the advertiser has provided ______________________________ for the program.

6. When many different advertisers buy random spots within a program but take no responsibility for the content of that program, they are engaged in ______________________ advertising.

7. Advertisers who purchase random spots in many different programs are engaged in

   ______________________________ buying.

8. Remote-control devices and videocassette recorders can both be used by viewers for

   ______________________________ unwanted commercials.

9. The placement of many short commercials in a single time slot creates

   ______________________________ that reduces the impact of commercials.

10. This problem is further aggravated by the practice called ________________________ that places separate messages for unrelated products in a 30-second spot.

11. Section 317 of the Communications Act of 1934 requires ________________________ to prevent deception about the source of program content.

12. Announcements placed at the beginning and end of programs that identify participating

    sponsors are referred to as ______________________________.

13. Each individual commercial in a designated time interval is called a

    ______________________________.

14. Programs that have no sponsorship whatsoever and are carried as a public service by stations and networks are called ______________________ programs.

15. FCC regulation requires stations to use time between programs (and between segments of longer programs) for ______________________.

16. Commercials for a station's own programming are called ______________________ whereas commercials designed to promote noncommercial organizations and causes are called ______________________.

17. Commercials of two, five, and even thirty minutes that explain or demonstrate a product are called ______________________.

B. *Sales, scheduling, and pricing*

1. The scheduling of commercials throughout the broadcast day is referred to as ______________________.

2. Cable delivers an ______________________ audience that is more prosperous and better educated than the general television viewer.

3. The measurement that relates the cost of a commercial to the size of its audience is ______________________.

4. Publications that give the cost of radio and television time on various stations are prepared by the ______________________ Service.

5. Advertisers who insist that their commercials be aired at a specific time purchase ______________________-position spots; advertisers who wish to have their commercials aired throughout the day purchase ______________________ spots.

6. These latter spots are given ______________________ rotation through different time periods and ______________________ rotation over different days of the week.

7. Advertisers willing to have spots cancelled and rescheduled in other time slots receive a lower rate to compensate for the ________________ risk they face.

8. Television salespeople frequently use a ________________ that allows them to quote different prices for the same spot and, consequently, gives them greater flexibility in negotiating contracts.

9. When several cable systems are interconnected, they are said to form a ________________ for advertisers who want to reach an audience throughout a geographic region.

10. Stations that sell commercial time for goods and services rather than for cash are involved in a practice known as ________________.

11. Quiz shows often give ________________ to compensate companies for the prizes they donate that are later awarded to contestants.

12. Sometimes stations will sell a block of time to ________________ who will then resell it to others.

13. A few stations will sell time to mail-order firms who agree to pay on a ________________ basis rather than at a set rate.

14. Most salespeople work from an account list, but some must create such a list by making ________________ calls to potential advertisers.

15. The ________________ provides selling aids for radio salespeople, and ________________ provides the same function for television salespeople. Cable salespeople get similar assistance from the ________________.

16. ________________ represent local stations and provide them with access to non-network national advertising.

17. The percentage of advertising dollars spent on various media is called the ________________.

18. ______________________________ receive a 15-percent commission on

______________________________ as payment for their responsibility in directing a total advertising campaign.

C. *Issues*

1. Programs are called ______________________________ when it is difficult to distinguish overall content from commercial messages.

2. Different names are used to identify those departments at networks and stations with responsibility for the review of programs and commercials. The three most commonly used titles include ______________________________, ______________________________, and ______________________________.

3. Prosecution for deception in advertising is under the jurisdiction of the ______________________________.

4. This agency has a ______________________________ Program to assure the correctness of an advertising claim.

5. That agency can seek a ______________________________ under which an advertiser agrees to stop a particular practice without admitting guilt.

6. Actual guilt must be proven before the agency can issue a ______________________________ order that has the force of law.

7. Some advertisers have even been forced to pay for ______________________________ that rectifies the messages contained in previous commercials.

8. ______________________________ is a consumer group concerned with advertising directed to children.

9. ______________________________, the practice where the star of a children's program delivers the commercial messages, is still discouraged by the FCC.

10. ______________________________ occurs when an announcer mentions a product on the air without telling the audience that he or she has a financial interest in that product.

11. ______________________________ involves the under-the-table payoff by record promoters to disc jockeys and others who prepare record playlists.

12. Local advertisers and stations sometimes conspire in a fraudulent practice called ______________________________ to charge manufacturers for spots that were never aired.

13. ______________________________ occurs when local stations cut away from network programming prematurely to insert their own commercials.

SELF-TEST

Fill in the Blank

1. Advertisers have the greatest control over the placement of their commercials when they ______________________________ entire programs.

2. Clutter undermines the ______________________________ of individual commercials within the sequence of nonprogram items.

3. Most sponsorship today is ______________________________ rather than true sponsorship.

4. Stations are required to make ______________________________ announcements at hourly intervals, but most do so more frequently.

5. Advertisers are reluctant to spend more money on cable advertising because the ______________________________ is inadequate.

6. The major factor that determines the amount a station can charge for each commercial spot is ______________________________.

7. Radio and television salespeople are generally paid on a ______________________________ basis.

8. The fee an advertising agency receives for creating and placing radio or television commercials is usually paid by ______________________________.

9. Under FCC regulations, what are the maximum number of commercial minutes a television station may air during one hour in prime time? ______________________________

10. ACT is greatly concerned about program-length commercials directed to an audience of

______________________________.

True/False

T F 1. Newspapers surpass television in total advertising volume, but television leads in national advertising.

T F 2. Both radio and television get over half of their income from network advertising.

T F 3. The term *sponsor* now means any advertiser, but it was once reserved for those who assumed responsibility for an entire program.

T F 4. Radio and television commercials are transient.

T F 5. Newspapers have greater flexibility to add advertising than do radio and television stations.

T F 6. Stations have finally resolved the clutter problem, and complaints by advertisers are declining.

T F 7. The Communications Act of 1934 prohibits anonymous sponsorship.

T F 8. Presidential addresses and state funerals are examples of sustaining programs.

T F 9. Surveys indicate that a majority of subscribers to HBO and other pay networks would not accept commercials under any circumstance.

T F 10. The CPM formula measures the cost of reaching a million households or people in a particular targeted group.

T F 11. ROS spots are generally more expensive than fixed-position spots.

T F 12. Preemptible spots frequently become make-goods.

T F 13. Plugs are legal when revealed but illegal when concealed.

T F 14. Per-inquiry advertising is most often carried on major television stations during prime time.

T F 15. Salespeople typically receive the highest pay among radio and television employees.

T F 16. Network sales staffs and national sales representatives are natural rivals because both are competing for TV dollars from national advertisers.

T F 17. Regulation of broadcast advertising is currently of greater concern to the FCC and the FTC than it has been in the past.

T F 18. The Television and Radio Codes of the National Association of Broadcasters are actively supported by the FCC and carefully followed by most broadcasters.

T F 19. Double billing occurs most frequently when networks and local stations attempt to bill advertisers for the same spots.

T F 20. Deregulation has removed the ban on payola.

PROJECT

Consult copies of *Standard Rate and Data* publications (see Exhibit 9.3) that deal with radio and television commercial charges. Which stations in your community have supplied information to these publications? Note how much various stations charge for time. If possible, try to locate similar information for cable systems and for newspapers.

CHAPTER 10

Other Economic Aspects of Electronic Media

CHAPTER FOCUS

Broadcasters and cable operate in a continually changing financial environment. Although the electronic media industry is a highly profitable one, not all stations and cable systems make money for their owners.

Programming is a large and continuing expense for broadcasters. Cable is a capital-intensive industry that requires operators to make a huge investment for initial equipment as well as continuing expenditures for maintenance. Electronic media, unlike print and film media, also require a sizable investment from consumers who must purchase and maintain the receivers needed to receive programs. For subscriber-supported services, further payments are required.

Public broadcasting has always suffered from insufficient funding. Government appropriations have not kept up with costs and public broadcasting must depend increasingly on subscriber donations and corporate underwriting.

CAPSULE

Main points from each section of Chapter 10 are summarized below.

10.1 Financial Framework

A. Television networks are both highly profitable and relatively immune from the financial ups and downs that affect most businesses. Television stations, both network-affiliated and independent, are also profitable (Exhibit 10.1). Although the majority of radio stations are profitable, a third did not show any profit according to a 1983 NAB study.

B. The cable industry is generally profitable, but profits and losses for multiple-system owners (MSOs) vary widely.

C. Home Box Office is the largest pay cable network. Pay cable growth has slowed, in part, because of competition from the videotape cassette recorder and the availability of first-run, unedited movies on videocassettes. Some pay cable networks suggest that VCRs enhance pay cable as subscribers record the movies provided by pay cable.

D. Few of the 40+ cable networks were profitable in 1986. Some networks have ceased operation; others have merged.

E. Large organizations such as group station owners and cable multiple-system owners are able to reduce costs through *economies of scale* and, subsequently, increase their profit margins. Operating costs for television stations and cable systems are relatively fixed; consequently, an increase in TV advertising or in the number of cable subscribers will greatly increase profits.

10.2 Program Economics

A. Most radio programming expenses are for personnel because distributors supply music to stations at no charge in exchange for the promotion their albums and tapes receive through air play. Television stations, however, spend enormous sums to acquire syndicated program series and feature films.

B. The typical radio station allocates 5 percent of its total expenses for news; for a network-affiliated television station, the figure exceeds 15 percent.

C. Broadcasters once considered news a necessary but unprofitable part of their business. Since 1963 some polls have identified television as the principal source of news for most Americans. Larger audiences have made news profitable as advertisers rush to buy time on news programs.

D. Local television program production is confined almost exclusively to news, weather, and sports programs.

E. About a third of all cable systems originate programming. Most programs are simple newscasts, information programs, and coverage of community events.

F. Television stations rely on syndicated programs to fill many broadcast hours. Programs are "rented" for a specific length of time. Fees are negotiated and are determined by such factors as the demand for the program, the size of the market, and the "newness" of the program.

G. Stations prefer syndicated programs that have 100 or more episodes. Because most such programs are initially produced for network airing at the rate of 22 per year, a network run of five or more years is needed to accumulate this quantity. The scarcity of these off-network series has forced stations to pay record-breaking prices for some of the more popular programs.

H. Stations acquire some programs on a barter basis. They pay no money for the programs but allow the syndicator to retain some of the commercial time slots.

I. Programs produced for network prime-time airing can cost as much as $1 million for each one-hour episode. Networks seldom pay that full cost and independent producers thus lose money on network showings. However, network airing enhances the value of the program for later syndication when the producer will recover the remaining costs and, hopefully, earn a handsome profit.

J. Production expenses are divided into two categories, *above-the-line* costs for the salaries of writers, performers, directors, and other creative personnel, and *below-the-line* costs for craft aspects such as scenery, costumes, and camera operators.

K. TV stations and networks consider on-air promotion announcements the most cost-effective way to advertise their programs. Some cable systems dedicate a channel to program listings or include printed program information when they send monthly bills. Both TV and cable provide information for newspaper program listings and for *TV Guide*.

10.3 Subscription and Other Supports

A. Cable system revenue comes primarily from the monthly fees paid by subscribers. All systems offer a *basic* service and most provide additional levels of basic and/or pay service called *tiers*.

B. Cable systems with *addressable converters* offer special programs on a *pay-per-view* basis. A few cable systems offer ancillary services such as home security protection.

C. Other fee-dependent media are multichannel multipoint distribution service (MMDS), satellite master antenna television (SMATV), and direct-broadcast satellite (DBS).

D. C-SPAN (Cable-Satellite Public Affairs Network) is neither wholly advertiser-supported nor dependent upon subscriber fees. It is supported by cable system operators who pay four cents or less a month per subscriber to carry the service.

E. FM radio stations can earn additional revenue or provide special services by utilizing their subcarriers. Some subcarrier services include Muzak, programming for the visually-impaired, foreign language programming, and information for paging systems (beepers). AM stations can multiplex inaudible secondary signals for power companies and other industrial users (Exhibit 10.2).

F. Television stations can utilize previously unused signal capacity for stereophonic sound or for simulcasts of foreign language audio. The vertical blanking interval can be used to transmit closed-captioned subtitles for the hearing-impaired and teletext.

10.4 Capital Investment

A. The most valuable asset of any radio or television station is the FCC license that permits operation of the facility. This license is of only potential value until the station owners acquire the equipment and facilities needed to transmit a broadcast signal.

B. The consumer must also make an investment—the purchase and maintenance of a radio or television receiver. The public's investment in receivers is estimated to be nine times as great as the broadcasting industry's investment in equipment.

C. On a cost-per-home-served basis, a cable system is more expensive to construct than a broadcast facility. The cost ranges from $600 to $1,200 per cable home. Costs of installing cable range from $10,000 per mile for aerial cable in rural areas to $100,000+ per mile for underground cable in urban areas.

D. Satellite transmission is widely used because it is more economical for long-distance signal relay than telephone lines or microwave. Users need not own entire satellites. Instead, they may own or lease a transponder. Satellite time can also be rented on a daily or hourly basis.

10.5 Buying and Selling Properties

A. Buying and selling of electronic media properties takes place on a continuing basis. Sales of radio and television stations, however, are always contingent on FCC approval of the license transfer. Before 1982 the FCC *trafficking* rules required a license holder to keep it a minimum of three years before transferring it. Now stations can be bought and sold as often as other media. Still remaining is the requirement that construction permits for new stations be held for one year before being transferred (Exhibit 10.3).

B. Station brokers handle most sales and generally receive a commission that is 5 percent of the selling price; commissions for major transactions are often at a lower percentage figure.

C. Although prices vary according to market size and a variety of factors associated with each station, there are some rules of thumb that are useful in estimating the price of a broadcast property. The price of an FM station or an AM/FM combination is usually about 2.5 times the station's annual gross revenue or 7.5 times its annual cash flow. For a stand-alone AM station, the figures are 1.5 times the gross revenue or 5 times its annual cash flow. For a television station, the rule is 2.5 times gross revenue or 10 times cash flow.

D. By 1986 the highest price ever paid for a radio station was $44 million for KJOI-FM in Los Angeles. KTLA-TV, also in Los Angeles, sold for $245 million in 1983 and sold for a record $510 million in 1985.

E. In 1985 each of the three major networks found itself the object of a takeover attempt – the first in more than three decades. Capital Cities Communication purchased ABC for $3.5 billion. General Electric (GE) purchased Radio Corporation of America (RCA), the parent company of NBC, for $6.28 billion. Ted Turner attempted a hostile takeover of CBS but was defeated by CBS management who fought successfully to maintain the corporation's independence (see Box).

F. Both Capital Cities/ABC and GE/NBC were required to sell certain broadcast properties to comply with FCC ownership regulations.

G. Cable systems are generally priced on a dollar value per subscriber. In the mid-1980s that value was $1,000 per subscriber or approximately $10 million for a system with 10,000 subscribers.

H. Two pay cable networks, Showtime and The Movie Channel, merged in 1983 in order to compete more effectively with HBO. Daytime and the Cable Health Network, two advertiser-supported services, merged to form Lifetime in 1984. In 1985 Viacom acquired full ownership of Showtime/The Movie Channel and of MTV, VH-1, and Nickelodeon. With these acquisitions, Viacom, which is also an owner of numerous cable systems and broadcast properties as well as a partial owner of Lifetime, became the largest cable programmer.

10.6 Funding Public Broadcasting

A. Although public broadcasting is noncommercial, stations do give credit in the form of underwriting acknowledgements to corporations that finance programs. Public broadcasters also raise money by selling goods at auction, selling production services, and even selling advertising in printed program guides (Exhibit 10.4).

B. Public broadcasters spend an inordinate amount of time in fund raising. Too many of their programs are bland and noncontroversial, designed more to avoid offending potential contributors than to provide a real alternative to commercial programs.

C. Various sources of long-range funding have been proposed for public broadcasting but none have been adopted. Several public broadcasting fund-raising acts have authorized federal funds for five-year periods but the actual authorizations were only for three years and were always for less than initially proposed. President Reagan said he supported the principle of public broadcasting, but he indicated the service should look more to the private sector and less to the federal government for funding.

D. The Temporary Commission on Alternative Financing for Public Telecommunications (TCAF) was created by Congress to test advertising as a funding device. Ten public television stations participated in a 15-month experiment with on-air advertising. The limited advertising added significant revenues and produced no negative impact on viewing patterns. There were certain unresolved questions and TCAF made no recommendations regarding the use of advertising on a continuing basis.

E. Program underwriting has become increasingly liberalized and increasingly controversial. Critics charge that the line between "enhanced" underwriting and commercials is dubious.

F. Individual members contribute about 20 percent of public broadcasting revenue. Stations conduct membership drives on the air, but polls show viewer resistance to this means of fund raising (Exhibit 10.5).

G. Other methods of raising funds for public broadcasting include (1) the selling of commercial rights to merchandise associated with programs such as *Sesame Street*, (2) the selling of programming to commercial television for initial showing before release to public television, and (3) a proposal before the FCC to allow exchange (for a cash payment) of a public broadcaster's more desirable VHF channel for a commercial operator's UHF channel in the same market.

KEY TERMS

A. *Financial framework and program economics*

1. When larger organizations purchase equipment, supplies, and even programs they are often able to negotiate a quantity discount that lowers the unit price of each item. This particular form of saving is known as ______________________ of ______________________.

2. ______________________ programs are those licensed on a station-by-station basis for local telecasting.

3. In a ______________________ deal, the station pays no money for a program but does give up some of the commercial time slots it would ordinarily sell to its own advertisers.

4. Independent producers often sell programs to networks for less than it costs the producers to make these programs. The term used to describe this practice is ______________________.

5. Production expenses relating to the creative aspects of production are called ______________________ and those incurred in the craft aspects are called ______________________.

B. *Subscription and other supports*

1. Local television services, local origination channels, and access channels are provided as a cable system's ______________________ service.

2. Additional levels of program service are called ______________________ and customers generally pay a separate fee for each level.

3. Home Box Office, Showtime, and Cinemax are all examples of ______________________ channels.

4. Cable systems with ______________________ converters offer special programs on a ______________________ basis that viewers can select on impulse.

5. Home Box Office, Cinemax, and other satellite-distributed program services encrypt or ______________________ their signals to prevent unauthorized reception.

6. FM stations may transmit Muzak and other types of specialized information on subcarriers. Collectively, these subcarrier services are known by the term ______________________.

C. *Buying and selling properties*

1. When broadcast group owners and cable multiple-system owners sell smaller, less desirable properties to buy larger ones, they are said to be ______________________.

2. In 1982 the FCC eliminated its 20-year old ______________________ rules that required a station owner to hold a broadcast license for a minimum of three years before transferring it.

3. AM radio stations that are not part of an AM/FM combination are referred to as

   ______________________.

4. A ______________________ occurs when the buyer of a corporation borrows most of the purchase price with the understanding that the debt will be repaid from future corporate revenue.

5. Showtime, MTV, and Nickelodeon are owned by ______________________.

D. *Funding public broadcasting*

1. Corporations that donate money to support specific programs on public television are usually given announcements or credits at the beginning and end of these programs. This

   practice is known as ______________________.

2. The term ______________________ is used to describe the need to protect the funding of public broadcasting from political pressures that may affect programming.

3. In 1981 Congress created a special panel called the ______________________ to evaluate the feasibility of using advertising as a funding device for public television.

4. The FCC now allows public television stations to sell announcements that allow a mention of product and location but do not allow a statement about product superiority.

   These "almost commercials" are referred to as ______________________.

5. In 1985 New York's WNET-TV began selling 30-second ______________________ announcements that include a company's logo, location, brand and trade names, and a description of the product or service.

6. A number of public television stations earn money from subscriptions and advertising associated with a tax-exempt multiedition program guide known as

   ______________________.

SELF-TEST

Fill in the Blank

1. The growth of pay cable has slowed, at least in part, because of competition from ______________ that allow owners the option of viewing unedited movies of their own choice.

2. Most of the programs produced by local television stations are in which content category? ______________

3. Program managers prefer to purchase off-network series that contain ______________ or more episodes.

4. One of the most successful magazines in America with 107 regional editions and a circulation of about 17 million is ______________.

5. Cable systems earn a limited amount of income from advertising but about 99 percent of their revenue comes from ______________.

6. The pay cable service with the largest number of subscribers is ______________.

7. Muzak, DataSpeed, and Physicians Radio Network all transmit information on that portion of the FM channel known as ______________.

8. In recent years which category of broadcast stations has declined rather than increased in value? ______________

9. In 1984 the FCC revised its "Rule of 7s." Now individual or corporate owners may own as many as ______________ stations in each category, but the TV stations may not reach more than ______________ percent of all U.S. television households.

10. In 1985 ABC was purchased by ______________ and NBC was purchased by ______________.

11. The individual who fought unsuccessfully to purchase CBS was ______________________.

12. One controversial method of raising money to support public broadcasting involves a limited type of sponsorship called ______________________.

True/False

T F 1. Most FM radio and UHF television stations are profitable today but only after years of losing money.

T F 2. The least profitable cable systems are those in larger cities where companies agreed to build expensive systems and charge unrealistically low subscriber fees.

T F 3. CBS Cable, a cultural programming channel, lost $30 million and was terminated by the parent corporation after only one year of operation.

T F 4. Radio stations spend a greater percentage of their expenditures on programming than do television stations.

T F 5. A study commissioned by the American Society of Newspaper Editors confirms the results of a study commissioned by broadcasters—that television is the primary source of news for the majority of Americans.

T F 6. Local stations will not buy a program until that program has completed its network run and the number of episodes in the series is clearly established.

T F 7. Most network programs do not make money for their producers until the programs reach the syndication market.

T F 8. One of the goals of *TV Guide* is to promote the television industry; consequently, the magazine offers little in the way of solid criticism.

T F 9. The cable Communications Act of 1984 grants franchising authorities the right to regulate for an indefinite period the rates cable systems can charge their subscribers.

T F 10. Only the largest organizations can utilize satellite transmission because the cost of purchasing a satellite is extremely expensive.

T F 11. Under current FCC regulations, a newly licensed broadcaster must own and operate a property for a minimum of three years before he or she can sell the station and transfer the license.

T F 12. One of the most common ways to price a cable system is to multiply the number of subscribers by a fixed figure which, during the mid-1980s, was approximately $1,000.

T F 13. Federal funding for public broadcasting increased substantially during the administration of President Ronald Reagan.

T F 14. The public television programs corporations are most eager to underwrite are those dealing with public affairs.

T F 15. Only 10 percent of the homes that watch public television contribute to the support of public stations.

PROJECT

Consult a recent copy of *Broadcasting* and read the section on "ownership changes" that is part of the larger division titled "For the Record" near the back of the magazine. Note the prices paid for various classes of stations. Also note the advertisements placed by communications brokers who are either listing broadcast properties or announcing transactions already completed.

PART 4

Programming

CHAPTER 11

Programming Problems, Processes, and Practices

CHAPTER FOCUS

A tremendous number of programs are required to fill the nineteen or more hours a day that most television stations broadcast. Most of these programs are produced by networks and syndicators; many are designed to appeal to specialized rather than generalized audiences. Cable networks must locate the movies and programs they need to fill their schedules.

Michael Dann, former CBS senior vice president for TV programming, believes that 50 percent of the reason for any program's success can be attributed to where it is placed in the broadcast schedule. This chapter discusses the strategies used by programmers to construct television schedules that maximize audience viewing of various programs.

CAPSULE

Main points from each section of Chapter 11 are summarized below.

11.1 The Problems: Program Shortage and Advertiser Appeal

A. Broadcasting and cable require a tremendous amount of programming. The term *parsimony* means an extreme economy of resources. Programmers apply the principle of parsimony when they rerun programs and when they use and reuse standardized content within programs. The radio disc-jockey format and the television soap opera and game show genres are examples of the latter.

B. Advertisers purchase radio and television time to address those segments of the population most likely to purchase their products. Consequently, many TV programs are designed to reach specific rather than generalized audiences. The target audience for afternoon soap operas is women in the 18 to 49 age range; the target audience for Saturday morning cartoons is children aged 6 to 15 or so.

C. Radio is even more segmented than television. Radio stations develop music-based formats that appeal to a particular audience segment and then solicit advertisers who want to reach this target audience.

D. Cable and public broadcasting also practice programming segmentation. One cable channel appeals to information seekers, another to sports fanatics, a third to the health-conscious. Many public television programs are targeted to middle- and upper-income viewers who provide financial support with voluntary subscriptions.

11.2 Program Production Processes

A. TV programs may be produced locally, or by a broadcast or cable network, or by a syndicator. Television stations produce local newscasts, occasional public affairs programming, and little else.

B. Most network and syndicated programming is produced in Hollywood by six major motion picture studios and by independent producers. Initially, the movie studios shunned TV; today they earn the majority of their revenue from the sale of theatrical motion pictures to television and from the production and distribution of television series (see Box in text).

C. Only a few new television series are produced each year and almost three-quarters of these are not renewed for a second season. TV series lose money during their network runs but usually make money through off-network syndication. Stations will generally not buy a series unless enough episodes have been produced to allow *stripping*—the airing of the program on a Monday-through-Friday basis during a given time period.

D. Although networks no longer produce entertainment programming, they do maintain separate news divisions that produce their own news and public-affairs programs. These divisions seldom accept news footage or documentary materials from outside sources.

E. Local news teams utilize electronic news gathering (ENG) to add live and taped coverage from on-the-spot sources to newscasts.

F. Both television and radio affiliates receive news items and features from their own networks. Independent television stations can receive news material from INN, UPITN, CNN, and other sources.

11.3 Changes in Entertainment Production Strategies

A. Cable, the VCR tape-rental market, and local television stations have increased their demand for movies (Exhibit 11.1). HBO alone requires 200 new movies a year. Hollywood has responded by doubling the number of movies produced annually from 120 in the late 1970s to over 250 in 1985.

B. Three trends in movie production and distribution are evident: an expanded release period, the popularity of sequels, and the broadening age range of the movie-going audience (see Box).

C. Movies have become increasingly expensive for the networks, particularly when compared to the ratings they generate. Both the full-service networks (ABC, CBS, NBC) and various ad hoc networks (Operation Prime Time, New Program Group) have developed less expensive made-for-television movies, prime-time specials, and miniseries.

11.4 Programming Practices

A. Radio and television stations and cable and broadcast networks share various common programming strategies.

B. Programmers break airtime into *day parts* (Exhibit 11.2). Radio day parts include morning drive, midday, evening drive, night, and overnight. Television day parts include daytime, early fringe, prime time, late fringe, and all other. Each day part has a predictable audience.

C. Program strategies attempt to control audience flow. The goal is to maximize *flowthrough* from one program to the next. Stations also work to gain inflow from and reduce outflow to competing stations.

D. Block programming maintains flowthrough by scheduling programs with similar appeal next to each other. Counterprogramming attempts to draw the audience away from a competitor's program by offering a different kind of program.

E. Programmers try to begin each day part with a program that will provide a strong lead-in for the programs that follow. New programs are often scheduled in *hammock* positions between two established programs that contribute audience to the new or weaker program.

F. Special programs, extra-long episodes, and schedule changes are examples of *stunting.* This strategy keeps competing networks off-balance and makes their own scheduling more difficult.

11.5 Scheduling Strategies

A. Network rivalry is the greatest during the 22 weekly hours of prime time. The cost of prime-time programming is so incredibly high that all three networks make more money with their daytime programming. Even so, each network's reputation, and its ability to charge top fees for advertising spots, is dependent on its performance during prime time.

B. Prime-time programs are usually scheduled on a once-a-week basis. Non-prime-time programs are generally *stripped* across the week on a Monday-through-Friday, or even a Monday-through-Sunday basis, as is the case with local news.

C. Affiliates air network programs about 65 percent of the time and fill the remaining 35 percent with local and syndicated programs. Independents must fill the entire day with local and syndicated programming. Consequently, they have much greater flexibility and can be particularly adept in counterprogramming their network affiliate rivals.

D. Both affiliates and independents use block programming (blocking), counterprogramming, and stripping to build their daily and weekly schedules.

E. Radio stations and cable systems and networks also use blocking, counterprogramming, and stripping. Radio stations often arrange program elements in hourly rotations, creating 60-minute content cycles that are modified by day-part strategies.

F. Cable pay networks such as HBO use *bridging*, a strategy that places a continuing program across a normal time break. For example, the viewer who chooses to watch the eight o'clock movie will probably still be watching at nine o'clock when programs on other channels are beginning.

11.6 Appraising the Program Services

A. Network television attempts to please all sorts of people at all times of the broadcast day.

B. Both radio and television are judged by the totality of their programming. Other cultural forms are judged by the individual efforts of specific artists and authors.

C. Although cable and other delivery systems have expanded the options available to viewers, the number of choices is still relatively low when compared to print media. Nevertheless, viewers with patience and foresight can usually find programs that suit their taste and interests.

KEY TERMS

A. *Terms relating to programming problems and processes*

1. When programs and program ideas are used to their fullest, we can say that radio and TV programmers are applying the principle of ______________________________.

2. When television audiences are segmented, the term ______________________________ is used to group audiences by age and sex. The term ______________________________ is used to group audiences according to their lifestyles and interests.

3. Many television and movie production companies are owned by larger firms with both media and nonmedia interests. These firms are known as ______________________________.

4. Motion pictures are released first to theaters, then via videocassettes, then to pay cable, then to network TV, and finally to local stations. Each distribution is for a specific period of availability called a ______________________________.

5. Television series with long runs accumulate the hundred or more episodes that local stations need when they purchase the series for ______________________________, the scheduling practice that puts a program in the same time slot every day of the week, Monday through Friday.

6. The miniaturization of cameras and the 1973 development of the time-base corrector has brought about a change in the way newscasts are produced. This new method is called ______________________________.

7. A syndicated news-program service, ______________________________, is now available for independent stations who want to offer a national newscast to their viewers.

8. Another syndicated service, ______________________________, provides international news and features for local stations to place within their own newscasts.

9. An ad hoc network that has produced and distributed several successful miniseries to nearly a hundred participating stations is ______________________________.

10. A group owner with television stations in the largest markets and a potential audience of one-sixth the television households is ______________________________.

B. *Terms relating to programming practices*

1. Both radio and television programmers divide each day's total airtime into

   ______________________________.

2. The evening period when television has the most viewers is called

   ______________________________.

3. The two periods immediately before and immediately after the period described above

   are called ______________________________.

4. The generalized movement of the audience from program to program and station to

   station is called ______________________________.

5. The audience a program acquires from the preceding program on the same station is

   called ______________________________.

6. The portion of the audience that leaves your station for a program on a competing

   station is called ______________________________. Conversely, that portion of the audience that leaves another station to view a program on your station is called

   ______________________________.

7. When you schedule a situation comedy opposite a competing station's newscast, you are

   employing a strategy known as ______________________________.

8. The scheduling of adjacent soap operas during an afternoon period is an example of

   ______________________________.

9. The placement of a very strong program at the beginning of a time period is called a

   ______________________________.

10. Special programming that disrupts the normal schedule and confuses competing networks

    is called ______________________________.

11. Scheduling a program across a normal time break is called ______________________________.

12. A ______________________________ was the phrase used by former FCC chairman Newton Minow to describe TV programming during the early 1960s.

SELF-TEST

Fill in the Blank

1. The most popular target audience for advertisers is ______________________________ who are ______________________________ years of age.
2. Lorimar, Tandem, and MTM are examples of ______________________________.
3. Generally, motion pictures are released on videocassettes after they have finished their exhibition in ______________________________ but before they are sold to ______________________________.
4. Network program production is limited to ______________________________.
5. Peak movie attendance occurs during the ______________________________ and the studios release many of their new films during this period.
6. The largest audiences for radio occur during ______________________________.
7. The first portion of TV prime time during which stations rather than networks provide the programming is called ______________________________.
8. The programming strategy that does the most to encourage audience flowthrough is called ______________________________.

True/False

T F 1. Programs that are original and unique illustrate the parsimony principle.

T F 2. Audience segmentation applies to commercial but not to public broadcasting.

T F 3. Several Hollywood movie studios are giving less attention to program production and more attention to program distribution and syndication.

T F 4. Independent producers can generally produce programs at a lower cost than can major studios.

T F 5. Network news organizations utilize news footage from a variety of sources to insure the most complete coverage of events.

T F 6. Electronic news gathering is very expensive and is used only by major market stations with sizable news budgets.

T F 7. Both independent and network affiliate stations carry the occasional miniseries produced by Operation Prime Time.

T F 8. Programmers create hammocks for their strongest programs.

T F 9. Prime-time programming gives all three networks their greatest profit margins.

T F 10. Independent stations have more scheduling options than do network affiliates.

T F 11. The programming strategy called bridging is most applicable to radio.

T F 12. Television and cable compare favorably with the public library because today's viewers have so many diverse program choices available to them.

PROJECT

Examine a copy of *TV Guide* or the weekly television listings in your Sunday newspaper. Find examples of programming blocks in both prime time and during other periods of the day. The noon, evening, and late-night news are obvious examples of stripping. What other examples can you find? How do the independent stations in your community counterprogram the network affiliates? How do the three networks counterprogram each other during prime time? Can you locate any hammocks that programmers have created to support new programs?

CHAPTER 12

Network Programs

CHAPTER FOCUS

Broadcast networks provide programming to their affiliates during 22 hours of prime time, many daytime hours, and into the late evening. Many cable networks provide programming to cable systems 24 hours each day.

Network programmers are always seeking novelty. Yet they approach new programs with caution because they are fearful that audiences will reject the unfamiliar. Various categories (or genres) of entertainment programming have been successful over the years. This chapter discusses some of these programs as well as some of the program producers.

Sports and news enjoy greater popularity with audiences today than ever before. Programming created specifically for children is limited in both quantity and quality. Network radio programming is restricted to brief newscasts and commentaries.

CAPSULE

Main points from each section of Chapter 12 are summarized below.

12.1 Distribution by Networking

A. All media content goes through cycles of invention, imitation, and decline. Nowhere is this more evident than in network television.

B. Network programmers seek novelty, yet network programming lacks diversity (Exhibit 12.1). Programmers want to be different, but they want to be so without taking chances.

C. Commercial broadcast and cable networks provide programming to affiliates that is structured to maximize audience flow and, thus, ratings. Affiliates benefit economically from network programming, and network advertisers benefit by gaining access to a nationwide audience in a single transaction.

D. Affiliates of the three commercial networks have little influence over network programming practices. In contrast, PBS affiliates determine network programming through the Stations Program Cooperative.

12.2 Prime-Time Entertainment

A. During the first three decades of network television, ABC, CBS, and NBC collectively shared 90 percent of the prime-time viewing audience. In the 1980s combined network share has declined to less than 80 percent because of competition from cable networks, improved programming on independent stations, and VCRs. This decline is expected to continue in the 1990s.

B. Network programs appeal to the largest possible audience, but they must also attract desirable demographic segments within that audience. Advertisers are most interested in reaching the midrange, upscale segment of the audience that accounts for the bulk of consumer spending.

C. ABC enjoyed a spectacular but short-lived success by emphasizing programs with strong youth appeal during the mid-1970s. NBC achieved success during the mid-1980s by allowing new programs, such as *Hill Street Blues* and *St. Elsewhere*, to build their audiences slowly.

D. Cost per-program-episode is also a consideration. Expensive programs with good ratings may be cancelled if less expensive programs are available.

E. Highly successful programs are often imitated with clones that copy the situation and plot of the original. Spin-offs are new programs built around familiar characters from established programs.

F. Situation comedies have long been a staple of prime-time network television and are also popular with syndicators (Exhibit 12.2). This genre showed signs of ratings slippage in the early 1980s, but was revitalized in the mid-1980s with the success of *The Cosby Show*, *Family Ties*, and *Cheers.*

G. Police dramas and detective shows (the action/adventure genre) have also proved successful in the mid-1980s.

H. The high cost of theatrical features has caused broadcast networks to turn increasingly to made-for-television movies and to miniseries. Pay cable networks (and especially HBO) use original made-for-pay movies to differentiate themselves from the broadcast networks and from each other.

I. Public television airs cultural and minority-interest programming that the commercial networks claim they cannot afford to schedule. Two cable networks, Bravo and the Arts & Entertainment Network, also carry such programming.

12.3 Non-Prime-Time Programs

A. Soap operas, game shows, and talk shows dominate daytime television just as they once dominated daytime radio. TV soap operas deal with more controversial topics than did radio, and soap fans are dedicated viewers. Game shows are inexpensive to produce and tend to have very long lives (Exhibit 12.3). Talk shows are also inexpensive, and the format is adaptable to a variety of topics and audiences.

B. With the success of MTV, video music has become a program genre. Now, other cable and broadcast networks utilize this form for entire programs and for portions of programs. The popularity of music videos may reduce the audience and the ratings for radio stations that play similar music.

12.4 The Role of Network Sports

A. Sports programming is important to network television because it attracts a middle-class male audience not reached by most other programs (see Box in text). However, the tremendous growth of sports coverage on both broadcast and cable networks has brought a decline in ratings and some decline in network interest.

B. Cable networks and independent stations find it easier to schedule live sports events than do broadcast networks and their affiliates. Many ad hoc networks exist to carry the games of a particular team or conference.

C. Sports producers have long been intrigued by the possibility of scheduling games on pay-per-view cable television and on large-screen theater television.

D. Certain ethical questions have been raised. One is the creation of commercial time-outs that artificially disturb the momentum of the game. Another involves scheduling of sports events to accommodate television coverage rather than the teams or their fans. A third asks whether television should regard sports as news and retain control of the coverage or regard it as entertainment and allow team-selected announcers to control the coverage.

12.5 Network Children's Programs and Other Educational Programs

A. The three commercial networks schedule six to seven hours of children's television each week. Nearly all of it is on Saturday morning; most of it is cartoons (Exhibit 12.5) and reruns of favorite sitcoms. This programming, which is sponsored by manufacturers of toys, cereals, and candies, represents good value for the networks because the time might otherwise go unsold.

B. PBS carries six critically admired weekend series, and Nickelodeon, a cable network, programs to different age groups of children.

C. Action for Children's Television, a consumer group, has complained about the low quality of children's programming. The group's 1971 petition to the FCC brought about extensive hearings. In 1974 the FCC rejected rule making but recommended voluntary improvements. Again in 1984, the commission rejected the call for rule making.

D. *Sesame Street*, the most widely acclaimed children's program, was launched in 1969 by the Children's Television Workshop, an independent, nonprofit corporation. CTW has also produced a reading series, *The Electric Company*, and a science series, *3,2,1 Contact.*

E. Instructional television for school-age children has had some success when used as a supplement to regular classroom instruction. Educational programming for adults is carried by public television stations and by satellite networks. Students can receive college credit for television courses they take through a cooperating university.

12.6 Network Television News

A. Although the audience for network entertainment is declining, the audience for network news and public-affairs programming is increasing. News operations are expensive to maintain and news programs generally lose money but earn visibility and prestige for their networks. The increased popularity of news has caused ABC, NBC, and CBS to expand their offerings. CNN now makes money with its 24-hour news coverage.

B. All three broadcast networks have proposed expanding their evening newscasts from 30 minutes to a full hour, but network affiliates have refused to yield time from their own highly profitable early-fringe schedules. The networks now schedule morning news or newsmagazine programs as well as short news summaries throughout the day and 1-minute micronewscasts between prime-time programs. ABC also schedules *Nightline* at 11:30 p.m. ET (Exhibit 12.6).

C. Cable News Network or CNN Headline News is carried by most cable systems. CNN has managed to attain equality with ABC, NBC, and CBS in determining rotation for pooled coverage and obtaining major interviews. CNN is able to provide live coverage of ongoing news events.

D. *The MacNeil/Lehrer Newshour* contains excellent in-depth coverage, but PBS affiliates have had difficulty finding the best placement for this program in their evening schedules.

12.7 Public Affairs

A. News documentaries are expensive to produce, rarely attract large audiences, and often cause controversy. Nevertheless, broadcasters and critics regard documentaries as evidence that television can be responsible and mature about serious matters. Current documentaries deal less with specific points and more with overall impressions.

B. The CBS series *60 Minutes* is a highly popular program and a ratings success. The magazine format allows the program to deal with a variety of subjects (Exhibit 15.1).

C. All three networks air public-affairs question-and-answer programs on Sunday. These programs have an impact that is measured more by the news value of the content than by the size of the immediate audience.

D. C-SPAN provides both live and taped public-affairs programming for its cable affiliates (Exhibit 15.4).

E. Television's coverage of momentous events such as the assassination of President John F. Kennedy, the Watergate controversy, the Vietnam War (Exhibit 15.5), and the famine in Ethiopia has a profound impact on the viewing public.

F. PBS carries more public-affairs programming than do ABC, NBC, or CBS. Nevertheless, critics fault PBS for its tendency to evade real controversy and they note that PBS underwriters have no more appetite for controversial programs than do advertisers on the commercial networks.

12.8 Radio Networks

A. News and public affairs form the primary content of network radio. News programs are generally limited to brief hourly newscasts and to commentaries (Exhibit 12.7).

B. ABC has created seven different networks, each with a distinctive style to complement the differing formats of various affiliate stations. Mutual offers its affiliates a highly popular over-the-night talk show hosted by Larry King.

C. National Public Radio has developed a distinctive late-afternoon news program called *All Things Considered* and a spin-off called *Morning Edition.*

KEY TERMS

A. *Entertainment programming*

1. When different television programs have similar form, content, or technique, they are said to belong to the same category or ______________________________.

2. Programs that appeal to two different groups within an audience are said to have a ______________________________ appeal.

3. Networks are less interested in attracting younger and older audiences and more interested in attracting the midrange ______________________________ segment of the audience that accounts for the bulk of consumer spending.

4. A new program that contains characters and a setting very similar to those in a popular, more established program is called a ______________________________.

5. When a familiar character from an established program becomes the dominant character in a new program, that new program is called a ______________________________.

6. *The Cosby Show*, *Family Ties*, and *Cheers* are all examples of a popular category of program known as ______________________________.

7. *Magnum P.I.* and *Miami Vice* are examples of a category known as ______________________________ programs.

8. Networks are using fewer theatrical movies and substituting less expensive ______________________________ movies to fill prime-time hours.

9. Home Box Office, Showtime, and other premium cable networks produce ______________________________ movies to distinguish themselves from the broadcast networks and from each other.

10. MTV has popularized a new form of visualized music called ______________________________.

11. ABC pioneered the ______________________________ format with *Wide World of Sports.*

12. Sports critics are concerned about the creation of ______________________________ that interrupt the normal flow of a televised football or basketball game in order to accommodate the TV network and its advertisers.

B. *Children's, educational, news, and public-affairs programming*

1. The cable network that features children's programming and programs certain hours for certain age groups is called ______________________________.

2. ______________________________ is the consumer group that persuaded the FCC to hold hearings about the status of, and the possible need for rules regarding children's television.

3. *Sesame Street* is produced by an independent nonprofit corporation known as the ______________________________.

4. Eleven midwestern universities have formed the ______________________________ to provide over-the-air courses for college credit.

5. The ______________________________ located at the University of Maryland has produced educational program series that appeal to both general and for-credit audiences.

6. Programs dealing with issues, problems, commentaries, editorials, panels, or documentaries fall under the broad category known as ______________________________.

7. Live coverage of the U.S. House of Representatives and coverage of other governmental bodies is provided to member cable systems by a cable network known as ______________________________.

8. National Public Radio is best known to listeners for its award-winning late-afternoon news program called ______________________________.

SELF-TEST

Fill in the Blank

1. Commercial network affiliates exercise ______________ influence over network practices and programming decisions. Noncommercial affiliates exercise ______________ influence over PBS practices and programming decisions.

2. During the 1980s, ABC, CBS, and NBC saw their collective share of the prime-time audience decline to less than ______________ percent.

3. ______________ enjoyed a spectacular although short-lived success as the network ratings leader in the mid-1970s by scheduling superficial situation comedies that emphasized sex and nostalgia.

4. ______________ became the network leader in the mid-1980s by allowing critically acclaimed programs to develop their audiences slowly.

5. PBS attracts a relatively large audience with ______________, a Sunday-evening program that features various miniseries produced in Britain.

6. What three program categories dominate daytime television? ______________, ______________, ______________

7. Popular music has been much more closely allied with radio than with television. However, the success of ______________, a cable network, has created an audience for videos on both cable and broadcast networks.

8. The principal owner of ______________, an all-sports cable network, is ______________.

9. When is most of the children's programming aired by commercial networks scheduled? ______________

10. In recent years, the size of the audiences for network news and information programs has been steadily ______________.

11. ________________________________ has achieved distinction as a highly popular public-affairs program and the only one from that category to become a ratings leader.

12. ABC operates ________________________________ different radio networks that provide formatted newscasts specifically designed to correspond to the presentation styles of the stations affiliated with each network.

True/False

T **F** 1. Most TV programmers are reluctant to take a chance on new programs that may not be immediately successful.

T **F** 2. In the early 1970s, CBS cancelled many high-rated programs because it wanted to change the demographics of its audience.

T **F** 3. Both *Dallas* and *Knot's Landing* are examples of TV program cloning.

T **F** 4. The competition for audience has made broadcast networks ever more willing to pay top prices for the TV rights to theatrical films.

T **F** 5. PBS has been criticized for filling so much of its schedule with British rather than American programs.

T **F** 6. Loyal soap opera viewers were irate when ABC cancelled some soaps and rescheduled others during the 1984 Olympics.

T **F** 7. Broadcasters control sports coverage because they, rather than the teams involved, control the hiring of play-by-play and color-TV announcers.

T **F** 8. The United States is one of the few countries that does not regulate the programming of children's television.

T **F** 9. Children's Television Workshop now earns about half its income from the sale of articles franchised to use the "Sesame Street" name and characters.

T **F** 10. University of Mid-America students can earn college credit for viewing television programs and completing related assignments.

T **F** 11. Dan Rather is the highest-paid performer on television.

T **F** 12. All three commercial networks are reluctant to expand their evening newscasts from 30 to 60 minutes.

T **F** 13. NBC's *News Overnight* and CBS's *Nightwatch* have been surprisingly successful in terms of audience size and advertiser sponsorship.

T **F** 14. *Meet the Press* and *Face the Nation* are two Sunday public-affairs programs that have greater impact than their meager ratings might suggest.

T **F** 15. National Public Radio provides 80 percent of the programming for its affiliate stations.

PROJECT

What are the top ten programs of the current television season according to the Nielsen ratings? (These ratings are usually reported in daily newspapers and also in *TV Guide*, *Variety*, and *Broadcasting.*) In what program categories or genres do these programs fit? Now take a look at all network prime-time programming. Do situation comedies seem to be gaining or losing audience appeal this season? How about action/adventure series? Can you identify any programs that are clones or spin-offs of other programs?

Compare the number and type of children's programs aired by your local PBS affiliate with the number and type of children's programs carried by any one of the commercial network affiliates.

CHAPTER 13

Nonnetwork Programs

CHAPTER FOCUS

Television stations that are network affiliates still need syndicated programming to fill many of the hours in their broadcast schedules. Independent stations use syndicated programming extensively. Programming supplied to affiliates and independents by syndicators may be either off-network or first-run. The prime-time access rule has created a sizable market for programs in the latter category.

Television stations are giving greater attention to local newscasts, which have become increasingly profitable as their ratings climb. But concern has been raised that local newscasts overemphasize short, "punchy" stories with exciting visual content.

Radio also utilizes syndicated programming. Some stations depend on format syndicators to supply their total music-programming needs. Other stations produce their own programming but buy supplementary items and series from feature syndicators.

CAPSULE

Main points from each section of Chapter 13 are summarized below.

13.1 Local Program Content

A. Individual stations produce less than 10 percent of all television programming, and almost all of this consists of news and public affairs. The other 90+ percent comes from networks and syndication.

B. Locally produced entertainment programming amounts to less than 1 percent of the total.

13.2 Distribution by Syndication

A. Syndicators sell both individual programs and program series to local stations. Stations prefer program series because they are easier to schedule and to publicize.

B. While programs are said to be *sold*, they are really only *leased.* Stations pay for the exclusive right to broadcast programs in a particular market during a specified period of time.

C. Many series have already been aired by one of the commercial networks and are available to local stations as *off-network* reruns. But many others are new programs available for *first-run* syndication. *M*A*S*H* is an example of the first category; *People's Court* an example of the second.

D. The FCC's prime-time access rule (see Box in text) requires network affiliates in the top fifty markets to broadcast new, nonnetwork programs during one hour of the four-hour prime-time period. (The FCC defines prime time as 7 p.m. to 11 p.m., ET.) Network affiliates choose to fulfill this obligation during the first hour which has become known in the industry as *access time.* Most affiliates favor first-run syndication over local production. Consequently, the prime-time access rule has given producers of first-run syndication a sizable market for the programs they create.

E. Independents and those network affiliates in smaller markets are free to select either first-run syndication or off-network reruns in addition to local production.

13.3 Off-Network Syndication

A. Affiliates schedule off-network series during the early fringe period and after the late news. Independents use them to counterprogram local news.

B. The series that do best in their initial network run are generally the ones that excel in syndicated rerun.

13.4 First-Run Syndication

A. Some first-run syndicated programs are expensively produced and are hardly distinguishable from network programming, but most are low-budget productions. Game shows and feature magazines (see second Box in text chapter) are popular access programs, in part because of their low cost.

B. Access programs may be bartered rather than sold. Syndicators obtain a series and presell some of the advertising slots. Then they syndicate the program to individual stations on a no-cost basis. The stations must agree to air both the program and the presold commercial messages. Stations can sell the remaining slots to local or national spot advertisers.

C. A few first-run programs and miniseries are broadcast in prime time by syndicators who create ad hoc networks for this purpose.

D. Stations, critics, and audiences have all complained about the limited number of high-quality syndicated programs and the consequent dreariness of nonnetwork programming. Nevertheless, the prime-time access rule has expanded production and encouraged diversity.

13.5 Local News

A. As the audience for local newscasts has grown, news has become increasingly important to individual stations. Both news department budgets and the length of the newscasts have increased dramatically. Local evening newscasts begin earlier and continue for sixty or even ninety minutes before giving way to network news. Some stations air local news both before and after the network newscasts, and in the largest markets local news extends to two or even two-and-a-half hours.

B. Because television is primarily an entertainment medium, many stations believe local newscasts must be entertaining to retain and increase audience size. News consultants have recommended "Happy Talk" and "Happy News" formats that are calculated to improve ratings. These formats are often combined with an *action-news* concept that emphasizes brevity in story length as well as a dependence on action-oriented visuals. Critics note that stories about accidents and fires invariably beat out such actionless but more important news as the economy and the energy crisis.

13.6 Cable Access Programming

A. Only 10 percent of the cable systems offer locally originated programs. Approximately half of these programs deal with public-affairs topics; the other half consist of entertainment or religion.

B. The localized nature of cable television is reflected in program content. Cable access programs serve a role in democracy by enabling taxpayers to see and hear local officials in action.

13.7 Syndicated Religious Programming

A. Fundamentalist preachers, long active in radio, extended their media coverage to television during the mid-1970s. Some even established their own cable networks (CBN, TBN, PTL) to distribute religious programming (Exhibit 13.1).

B. Although religious programs are classified as syndication, the usual financial aspect of the syndication transaction is reversed. Stations do not pay the evangelists for the programming; rather, evangelists pay stations for the airtime.

C. Some fundamentalist preachers intermix religion and politics. They use their radio and television ministries to advocate conservative views on a variety of political issues.

13.8 Other Types of TV Syndication

A. Various cable networks (USA, WTBS) fill large portions of their schedules with off-network series, barter specials, and some first-run syndication.

B. Instructional and educational programming for children and adults is available from noncommercial syndicators. These nonprofit agencies license program series for broadcast by public television stations.

13.9 Radio Syndication

A. The use of syndicated material by radio stations varies widely. Some stations use a few short features and specials; others use syndicator-supplied programming to fill the entire broadcast day. Syndicators deliver their materials on tape, but many are now shifting to satellite distribution.

B. Over half the radio stations use some degree of automation. Syndicated music formats are easily used with automated systems (Exhibit 13.2).

C. Format syndicators supply total programming in a variety of formats according to station need. Feature syndicators supply program items designed to fit within particular formats. Two of the better-known feature series are Dick Clark's *Top 40 Countdown* and Casey Kasem's *American Top 40.*

13.10 Radio Formats

A. Although radio is characterized as a local medium, its principal programming ingredient is nationally distributed recorded music. Consequently, a Top-40 station in Portland, Maine, will be playing the same music as a Top-40 station in Portland, Oregon.

B. Radio formats are built around different categories of popular music. The most popular format is rock; the second most popular format is country. Each of these formats has variations, such as adult-contemporary rock, album-oriented rock, or urban country. Some other commercial formats include easy listening, beautiful music, nostalgia, soul, and classical (Exhibit 13.3).

C. Less than 10 percent of radio stations utilize *news/talk* and *all-news* formats. Another 3 percent use a two-way-telephone talk format. News and talk stations generally broadcast on the AM band.

D. During the 1960s, some stations developed a less rigid style of programming called *underground* or *free-form* radio. Five stations owned by the Pacifica Foundation have been relatively successful with this concept (see third Box).

E. Classical music and jazz are the two formats used by most noncommercial radio stations. Both represent alternatives to the common commercial formats.

KEY TERMS

A. *Television programming*

1. Many programs and series initially broadcast on network television are then sold to local stations for additional airing. These programs are called ______________________ syndication.

2. Programs that have never been broadcast are also sold to local stations. These programs are called ______________________ syndication.

3. When a program series is sold to a station, an ______________________ clause in the sales agreement guarantees the station that it will be the only one with access to the series in that market.

4. Syndicators display their programs at the annual convention of the ______________________.

5. Much of the market for syndicated programming was created by the FCC's ______________________ Rule.

6. The hour from 7 p.m. to 8 p.m. Eastern Time is referred to as ______________________.

7. The distribution system that requires programs on tape to be physically transported from one station to another is called ______________________________.

8. Stations need not pay to air certain programs that include a specified number of presold advertising spots. These programs are an example of ______________________________ syndication.

9. In local newscasts, the informal banter among members of the on-air news team has become known as ______________________________.

10. Stories that lack news value but give the viewer a positive feeling about the newscast are called ______________________________.

11. Frank N. Magid Associates and McHugh-Hoffman are two of the best known ______________________________.

12. The label ______________________________ describes a news presentation style that emphasizes brevity and visual impact.

13. A highly commercialized approach to religious broadcasting has brought many viewers and listeners to a new place of worship called the ______________________________.

14. The first of the major evangelists to exploit the resources of television was ______________________________.

15. The fundamentalist minister who is outspoken in his political views and regularly buys time on commercial television for his syndicated programs is ______________________________.

16. ______________________________, the president of CBN and the star of *The 700 Club*, is often cited as the best example of the newer and highly effective TV evangelists.

17. Another evangelist, ______________________________, hosts *The PTL Club* and insists that any attempt to question his financial operations is an invasion of the constitutionally guaranteed freedom of religion.

18. Two noncommercial syndicators who supply educational and instructional programs to public television stations include the ______________________________ and the ______________________________.

B. *Radio programming*

1. MOR radio stands for ______________________________ and appeals to an ______________________________ demographic group.
2. A ______________________________ music format is very popular with rural listeners but less popular with urban listeners.
3. Because much of the work in the program, production, and business departments of radio stations is repetitive, many stations are turning to ______________________________ systems that require fewer personnel.
4. Some stations purchase their entire music programming from ______________________ who supply a full 24-hour schedule of material.
5. Other stations prefer to purchase more limited programming from ______________________________ who supply package items that can be interwoven with locally produced material.
6. ______________________________ is the most common music format for successful stations in the top fifty U.S. markets.
7. The broad-appeal format that combines orchestrated music with popular songs is called ______________________________.
8. Stations that play little or no music and emphasize news, interviews, and talk refer to themselves as ______________________________ stations.
9. ______________________________ stations are the most expensive to program and are only successful in large cities. These stations use a revolving-door programming principle that delivers repetitive material in 20-minute blocks.

10. Five stations supported by the ______________________ Foundation have developed a nonformat type of programming called ______________________ radio.

SELF-TEST

Fill in the Blank

1. The most important locally produced program for most television stations is ______________________.

2. The prime-time access rule limits network programming to a maximum of ______________________ hours during the 7 p.m. to 11 p.m. period (Eastern and Pacific time).

3. The syndicators of timely programs such as *Entertainment Tonight* use ______________________ to distribute their products to client stations.

4. The most common category of programming by local cable systems involves ______________________.

5. Most religious broadcasters come from ______________________ rather than mainstream denominations.

6. Format syndication is particularly popular with radio stations that have ______________________ systems.

7. Although there are many variations, the most popular radio format utilizes some form of ______________________ music.

8. The two musical formats most popular with noncommercial radio are ______________________ and ______________________.

True/False

T F 1. *Entertainment Tonight* and *People's Court* are two of the best-known off-network syndication programs.

T F 2. Syndicated programs are never really sold but instead are leased for a stipulated number of "runs" over a fixed period of time.

T F 3. Since 1973 the FCC has barred ABC, CBS, and NBC from involvement in the syndication of television programs.

T F 4. Most barter programs are either off-network or daily first-run series.

T F 5. Television stations in major markets limit early-evening local newscasts to thirty minutes so that more time will be available to air profitable, syndicated programming.

T F 6. Critics of local television news express strong support for those news consultants who use psychological tests to analyze public perception of news content and station personnel.

T F 7. The airtime used for most religious broadcasting is provided without charge by the stations that carry these programs.

T F 8. Viewers of religious television more frequently tend to be female, nonwhite, older, less educated, and have lower incomes than the general television audience.

T F 9. Radio stations continually change formats in an attempt to stay abreast of musical trends.

T F 10. Drake-Chenault Enterprises and Bonneville Productions are two of the most successful radio-format syndicators.

T F 11. Block programming in radio uses several different formats, each suited to a different day part.

T F 12. Most underground or community radio stations are highly profitable commercial enterprises.

PROJECTS

What programs do the television stations in your community air during the "access time" period? Which program is the ratings leader during the first halfhour? Which leads during the second half-hour?

Does any station in your community call its local newscast *Action News*? How does that newscast differ from newscasts aired by competing stations?

Describe the formats of at least ten radio stations that broadcast in or near your community. Which stations do you listen to and why?

PART 5

Effects

CHAPTER 14

Audience Measurement and Testing

CHAPTER FOCUS

Different media measure audiences in different ways. Print media use circulation figures whereas the motion picture industry calculates movie attendance and box office receipts. It is much more difficult to tabulate the continually changing audience for the programs on commercial radio and television.

Broadcast ratings are usually considered a measure of program popularity, but they are also financial measurements. It is the size and composition of an audience that determines how much broadcasters can charge advertisers for commercial time. Both broadcasters and advertisers depend on research organizations such as Arbitron and Nielsen to provide this information.

This chapter explains how ratings data are collected and interpreted. It also discusses certain nonrating research that is used by broadcasters and advertisers to test program and advertising concepts.

CAPSULE

Main points from each section of Chapter 14 are summarized below.

14.1 The Ratings Business

A. The public is very aware of broadcast ratings; it is much less aware of magazine and newspaper circulation and readership surveys. Audience measurement in broadcasting and cable is unique because, unlike print media, there is no readily countable physical output.

B. Arbitron and Nielsen are the two firms that dominate broadcast media research. Arbitron provides localized data for 214 local television markets and for 260 local radio markets. Nielsen provides nationwide data for the television networks and localized data for 205 local television markets. The network television data are compiled and reported continuously; the market-by-market television and radio data are gathered in short spurts known as *ratings periods* or *sweeps.*

C. Local ratings reports are used by stations to sell time to advertisers and to evaluate their own programming and that of the competition (Exhibit 14.1). ABC, CBS, and NBC make similar use of the network reports (Exhibit 14.2).

D. Both Arbitron and Nielsen publish supplementary reports dealing with syndicated programming, minority audience preferences, and ratings trends. Clients may order special reports tailored to specific needs.

14.2 Collecting Set-Use Data

A. Diaries, meters, and telephone interviews are the principal ways used to collect ratings data. Each method has advantages and disadvantages.

B. Diaries are used for market-by-market surveys that require relatively large samples. Diaries are inexpensive, but they require active and accurate participation by the individuals in each sample (Exhibit 14.3).

C. Meters are used for the nationwide measurement of network programming provided by Nielsen and for the overnight measurements provided by both Nielsen and Arbitron in selected major markets. Data from the meters are transmitted by telephone line to data-processing centers in Dunedin, Florida, (Nielsen) and Beltsville, Maryland (Arbitron). Meters are quite expensive but give the most accurate measurement of set use. They do not, however, reveal audience composition or even audience presence (Exhibit 14.4).

D. Telephone interviews are relatively inexpensive to conduct. The interviews may be coincidental or recall. *Coincidentals* provide momentary data by asking only about set use at the time of the call. *Recall* interviews ask about set use over a longer period of time. Recall interviews provide many more data, but the data are less accurate because they depend on the memory of the respondent. Nielsen uses coincidentals to collect information for special reports. RADAR uses telephone recall interviews to gather data for radio network ratings.

E. Both Nielsen and Arbitron (as well as another firm, AGB) are experimenting with *people meters* that provide data about individual rather than household viewing habits. The Arbitron "ScanAmerica" meters can also be used to read electronically the product codes of new purchases. Thus, viewing and buying behavior can be correlated (Exhibit 14.5).

14.3 Ratings Concepts

A. Each of the more than 3,000 counties in the United States is assigned to one television market (Exhibit 14.7). Arbitron calls these markets "Areas of Dominant Influence" or *ADI*s; Nielsen uses the term "Designated Market Areas" or *DMA*s.

B. The elementary sampling unit in television is the household; in radio, it is the individual.

C. A *rating* is an estimate of the percentage of households tuned to a particular program at a given time (Exhibit 14.6). Let's assume that a sample of 400 households is chosen to represent the 100,000 households in a particular community. One hundred, or 25 percent, of the households in the sample are tuned to a particular program. The rating for that program is 25, and the projected audience is 25 percent of the total households or 25,000 households.

D. Prime-time television programs average a 17 rating; daytime programs average a 6.

E. *Households using television (HUT)* is the percentage of homes tuned to some station during any one time period. If the HUT is 55, then 55 percent of the homes are tuned to something; the remaining 45 percent are not using television during this time period.

F. HUT levels vary by day part, averaging 25 for daytime hours and 60 for prime-time hours. HUT levels also vary by season and by day of the week.

G. *Share* is the percentage of homes using television (or radio) that are tuned to one particular station. In the example above, we noted that 100 of the 400 homes were tuned to one program. Let's assume that another 100 are tuned to all other programs and the remaining 200 are not using television. Share is calculated by dividing the number of households viewing a particular program by the number of households using television. In this case, the 100 households tuned to a specific program are divided by the 200 homes tuned to all programs and the share is 0.50 (50 percent) or simply 50 (Exhibit 14.6).

H. Share percentages are used as programming tools. They tell managers how well specific programs are doing in the competition for audience. Ratings are used as sales and advertising tools. They give both sales personnel and advertisers an estimate of how many households are viewing certain programs and, consequently, are being exposed to certain commercial messages.

I. Because the radio audience is fractionized among so many stations, radio ratings are very small—rarely more than 2 or 3. Radio stations and their advertisers use cumulative audience figures as well as ratings and share. These *cumes* tell how many different people have tuned to a radio station at least once over a period of several days or even in a week. *Reach* is another term for cume.

J. Ratings books also report audience composition in terms of gender and age categories. These *demographics* are of particular interest to advertisers who want to direct their commercial messages to those groups most likely to buy their products (Exhibit 14.8).

14.4 Sampling

A. Sampling involves the collection of data from randomly selected representatives of a specific population. Various methods are used to ensure that the selection is truly random and that the characteristics of the sample correspond to the characteristics of the population under study (Exhibit 14.7).

B. Higher reliability is achieved by using a larger sample. The reliability increases in relation to the square of the sample size. To double the reliability, you must quadruple the size of the sample. Researchers and clients balance the level of reliability and the degree of sampling error they are willing to accept with the amount of money they are willing to spend to collect the data.

14.5 Broadcast Audiences

A. Nearly all homes in America have both radio and television receivers. The potential broadcast audience is over 84 million households.

B Although television is no longer a novelty, HUT levels have not declined as some observers predicted. Instead, HUT levels have continued to climb. They consistently reach 70 percent during the top prime-time hour from 9 p.m. to 10 p.m.

C. Viewer behavior is often governed by a decision to simply watch television rather than a decision to watch a particular program. Having made the first decision, viewers are willing to accept the *least objectionable* of the program choices available to them.

D. Closely related to choosing the least objectionable program is the concept of *tuning inertia.* Viewers tune to one station and remain with it for an extended period. Tuning inertia can also be applied to radio. Most listeners confine their tuning to two or three favorite stations.

E. Demographic variables can be used to predict viewing habits. Women view more TV than do men. Among adults, viewing increases with age but decreases with education. Other variables are also predictive (Exhibit 14.8).

F. Demographic variables can also be used to predict radio format preference. Contemporary music formats appeal to those in their teens and twenties; news and talk formats appeal to older listeners.

14.6 Audiences for Cable and Newer Media

A. Broadcast research techniques are being applied to cable, but some problems arise. One is the difficulty in measuring an audience that is fractionized across so many channels. Another is the limited ability of cable networks, systems, and advertisers to pay for expensive ratings services (Exhibit 14.9).

B. Videocassettes are used for timeshifting (Exhibit 14.10), but this presents problems for audience researchers. What kind of audience composition should be credited to a program recorded when no one is home? What credit should be given when replays occur weeks later? What about multiple replays?

14.7 Use and Abuse of Ratings

A. The Electronic Media Rating Council (EMRC), an independent auditing agency, accredits ratings services that meet established standards. It also ensures full disclosure of the methods used to compile and interpret data.

B. Networks and stations abuse ratings when they ignore sampling error and treat the figures as precise measurements rather than as estimates.

C. Ratings tend to overestimate the broad middle-range majority and underrepresent the very rich, the very poor, and ethnic minorities. In recent years, both Arbitron and Nielsen have made special efforts to get minority respondents in their samples to participate fully.

D. Stations and networks often make deliberate attempts to influence or "hypo" the ratings by airing extraordinary programming or by engaging in promotional efforts (stunting) during ratings periods. This practice is particularly evident during the November and February television sweeps.

E. Critics argue that the "quantitative" ratings system now in use encourages mediocrity and favors the "least objectional" over the best possible programs. Public broadcasting has worked to establish "qualitative" ratings, but commercial broadcasters have little interest in or use for such a system.

14.8 Nonrating Research

A. Nonrating research tries to find out what people like and dislike, what they recognize and remember. Both program and advertising concepts may be tested for public approval early in the development stage.

B. Some researchers measure involuntary physical reactions such as pulse rate or pupil dilation to determine how audience members react to given stimuli.

C. Researchers sometimes use test markets to measure the effectiveness of advertising and its influence on product sales.

D. While attention is given to viewers and listeners who telephone or write to express opinions about programs or commercials, these "activists" are not statistically representative of the entire audience, and the opinions they offer may be misleading.

KEY TERMS AND NAMES

A. *Collecting data*

1. Since 1914 the ______________________________ has assisted advertisers by verifying the sales and distribution of newspapers and magazines.

2. Which company provides ratings for both radio and television stations?

   ____

3. Which company provides ratings information about the audience for network television as well as the audience for individual television stations? ______________________________

4. Four times a year the ratings firms survey all television markets and provide local stations and their advertisers with detailed information about audience composition. These periodic surveys are called ______________________________.

5. ______________________________ is a relatively new firm that supplies monthly reports and quarterly summaries in 125 radio markets.

6. Statistical Research, Inc., operates a national radio network ratings service called ______________________________.

7. Several methods are used to collect the set-use data that are required to compile ratings. The method that places the most responsibility on viewers and listeners involves the keeping of ______________________________.

8. Which method provides the most precise information about television use but no information about audience composition? ______________________________

9. The oldest method of gathering data and one that gives relatively accurate information, but for a very limited time period, involves the use of ______________________________ surveys.

10. The company that issues radio network ratings uses the ______________ method to gather data over a seven-day period.

11. This company employes a technique called ______________ to generate a random sample and ensure that all elements of the population are represented.

12. Audience researchers are placing more emphasis on individual viewing and listening habits. Special ______________ are being developed to record these kinds of data.

B. *Ratings concepts*

1. Arbitron uses the term ______________ to designate each of its 214 local television markets.

2. Nielsen uses a similar term ______________ to designate its 205 local TV markets.

3. In audience measurement, researchers must define the single entity or ______________ that will be counted when the data are collected.

4. With TV ratings, the single entity most commonly used is the ______________.

5. The percentage of television households tuned to *some* station during a particular time period is called ______________ or simply the ______________ level.

6. The percentage of the *total possible audience* that is tuned to a particular program is called the ______________.

7. The percentage of *households using television* that is tuned to a particular program is called the ______________.

8. The percentage of the total possible audience that tunes to a particular station at least once during an extended time period (perhaps several days or a week) is called a ______________ audience figure or simply a ______________.

9. ______________________________ is another term for the answer to the previous question.

10. In addition to total audience figures, audience composition is reported in terms of gender and age. These subgroup measurements are called ______________________________.

C. *Sampling and audience concepts*

1. It is just not feasible to measure everyone's viewing and listening habits. Therefore, ______________________________ procedures are used that allow the activities of a few to represent the larger population.

2. These representatives must be chosen through a ______________________________ selection process or the procedure will be flawed.

3. The probable amount of statistical uncertainty in the measurement can be calculated in advance and is known as the ______________________________.

4. The term ______________________________ is used to describe errors that occur because the wrong questions are asked, the wrong respondents are chosen, or other mistakes have occurred in the measurement process.

5. The percentage of individuals or households in a sample who agree to participate in the measurement process is called the ______________________________.

6. ______________________________ sampling occurs when members are drawn from specific subgroups to ensure that the composition of the sample is similar to the composition of the population under study.

7. A similar corrective can be applied to data after collection by ______________________________ the data obtained from certain sample members.

8. Set ______________________________ refers to the percentage of all homes that have broadcast receivers. That figure has long been between 98 and 99 percent.

9. Paul Klein has suggested that TV viewers often select the ______________________________ because they simply feel like watching TV.

10. The tendency for viewers and listeners to remain with the same station over an extended period is called ______________________________.

D. *Other measurement concepts*

1. Cable ______________________ refers to the percentage of all homes that subscribe to a cable service.

2. When audiences use videocassette recorders for ______________________, a ratings firm must determine when and how the audiences will be credited to the programs being viewed.

3. Four times a year, Nielsen issues a special ______________________ Report that provides audience data on national cable networks and pay cable services.

4. The ______________________ accredits specific ratings services that meet certain standards and submit to annual auditing.

5. In research, the term ______________________ refers to the dependability of the measurement and the term ______________________ refers to the degree that the data actually measure what they purport to measure.

6. ______________________ is the term used to describe attempts by stations to influence their ratings with extraordinary programs or promotional efforts during measurement periods.

7. Critics of the present ratings system believe that ______________________ ratings should be developed to measure audience loyalty and interest as well as audience size.

8. Some attitudinal research methods utilize small panels of individuals to discuss their reactions to certain programs. These panels are called ______________________.

9. Minute-by-minute reactions to a program can be processed by a device called a ______________________ that enables test group members to express their reactions by pressing one of several buttons at various intervals.

10. Involuntary physical reactions to program stimuli might include changes in brain waves, eye movements, pupil dilation, and pulse rate. All of these measurements fall under the broad category of ______________________ testing.

11. While psychologists question the effectiveness of the technique, the FCC has nevertheless banned the use of ______________________ advertising that utilizes very brief messages designed to have an unconscious impact on members of the audience.

SELF-TEST

Fill in the Blank

1. Arbitron and Nielsen derive most of their ratings revenue from the sale of reports to

   ____________________ and ____________________.

2. The three main ways of collecting ratings data include ____________________,

   ____________________, and ____________________.

3. How quickly are the TV ratings data collected in the largest markets available for use?

   ____

4. Both ADI and DMA are used to define each of the 200+ television ____________________ in the United States.

5. For television the elementary sampling unit is ____________________, whereas

   for radio the elementary sampling unit is ____________________.

6. Both a ratings and a share are reported for each program. Generally, programmers are more

   interested in the ____________________, and sales managers give more attention

   to the ____________________.

7. Television viewing increases throughout the day and peaks during the top prime-time hour from 9 p.m. to 10 p.m. During that period the HUT level is generally about

   ____________________ percent. Average viewing per household is more than

   ____________________ hours each day.

8. Reliability and sample size are related. To double the reliability, the sample size must be

   increased by a factor of ____________________.

True/False

T F 1. The audiences for newspapers, magazines, and movies are less difficult to measure than the audiences for broadcasting and cable.

T F 2. Arbitron is the only company that provides ratings for both radio and television.

T F 3. Diaries provide the most accurate measurement of set use but are also the most expensive method of collecting data.

T F 4. People meters can provide data that allow researchers to correlate viewing and buying behavior.

T F 5. Each county in the United States is assigned to *one* ADI/DMA.

T F 6. The ratings of a program is always larger than its share.

T F 7. "Reach" is another term for cume.

T F 8. It is simply not possible for only 1,700 randomly chosen homes to estimate the tuning behavior of 84 million households.

T F 9. Known biases can be reduced by weighting certain data.

T F 10. Radio listening reaches its highest peak during morning drive time.

T F 11. The heaviest viewers of television are teen-agers and college students.

T F 12. Cable audience measurement is less concerned with the audience for basic cable services than with the audience for HBO and other pay services.

T F 13. Arbitron and Nielsen have angered critics by refusing to reveal the methods used to collect data and calculate the ratings.

T F 14. Focus groups are of no value in ratings research but of considerable value in attitudinal research.

T F 15. Information obtained from letters and phone calls can give broadcasters a representative sample of audience attitudes and opinions.

PROJECT

Get together with four or more of your friends and form a focus group to discuss the content of certain programs. If you have access to a videocassette recorder, record the programs and play them back as part of the focus group analysis. Otherwise, choose programs that are thoroughly familiar to all members of the group.

Begin with a local news program. Do you feel the anchors and reporters are believable? Did the newscast give proper emphasis to the stories you think are important? What about the style of presentation?

Now move to one or more situation comedies. With which characters do you most closely identify? Why? Are the story lines believable?

Select another entertainment format and perform the same sort of program/audience analysis.

CHAPTER 15

Social Consequences

CHAPTER FOCUS

Can the American public spend a tremendous amount of time watching television and listening to radio and not be heavily influenced by these media? What are some of the effects of television and radio on different members of the audience? How can these effects be measured? These are some of the questions raised in Chapter 15. As you might expect, it is impossible to answer these questions with any degree of certainty. Research in mass communication attempts to probe these questions and develop theories that explain, at least in part, the varying impact of different categories of content. This chapter discusses the consequences of advertising, news, political content, and entertainment. Special attention is given to the inclusion of violence as an integral part of television content and the impact of that violence on TV viewers.

CAPSULE

Main points from each section of Chapter 15 are summarized below.

15.1 Approaches to Research

A. Research on the impact of media usually focuses on the medium of greatest importance at the time. Most of the research conducted between 1930 and 1950 dealt with radio and motion pictures. Since 1950 the overwhelming majority of research has dealt with television.

B. No single unifying theory of mass communication has emerged. Researchers have attempted to understand the process of communicating. Various models have been constructed in an effort to identify the elements within the process and to explain the interrelationship of these elements.

C. The *effects model* suggests that media content directly affects behavioral outcome. During the 1960s, researchers concluded that this effect was minimal since media content is only one among many factors and influences. During the 1970s, opinion began to shift away from this *minimal-effects* concept, primarily because of intensive research conducted on the effects of media violence.

D. The *uses-and-gratifications model* places more emphasis on process than content. Media are assessed in terms of what individual audience members do with media rather than what the media do to audiences. The model notes that people use media in different contexts and emphasizes people-media interactions. It recognizes the importance of entertainment, the major element in media content.

E. The *accommodation model* is the most complicated of the three. It places greater emphasis on what individuals bring to the communication process. Personal experience and interpersonal contacts influence what individuals learn from the media.

15.2 Methods of Studying Consequences

A. Listener and viewer responses supply the data for media research. Data gathering, whether based on self-reporting or direct observations, introduces an element of artificiality or intrusiveness into the media setting.

B. Survey data, such as those collected in opinion polls and audience ratings, yield information about behavior but tell us nothing about the causes of the behavior.

C. Content analysis examines the content of communication materials and quantifies whatever features interest the researcher. Both the nature and source of the content categories are determined by the researcher.

D. Laboratory experiments enable researchers to control experimental factors and to exclude extraneous events and influences. Lab experiments put people in artificial settings that bear little resemblance to real-life situations.

E. Field studies enable the researcher to observe behavior and collect data in a more realistic setting.

F. Field experiments attempt to combine the control of the laboratory experiment with the natural setting of the field study. They are, however, both costly and difficult to arrange.

15.3 Consequences of Advertising

A. Advertising pays the entire direct cost of radio and television. Consumers eventually pay this cost indirectly because advertising expenses are added to the price of consumer goods and services.

B. Critics claim that advertising persuades consumers to want and eventually purchase items for which they have no real need.

C. Advertising practitioners note the limited power of advertising and cite as evidence the failure of many new, highly advertised products. Much advertising is designed to build and retain brand loyalty.

D. Consumer groups believe that advertising directed to young children takes unfair advantage of a group that is not always able to recognize the purpose of advertising or to separate the advertisements from program content.

15.4 News Impact

A. News personnel perform a *gatekeeping* role when they select and position the items contained in a news presentation. The visual bias of television news (1) favors stories that make good pictures and (2) attempts to illustrate nonvisual stories with irrelevant visual material.

B. Closely related to gatekeeping is *agenda setting.* This overall process of selecting and ranking events and issues over the longer term is a prime determinant of public opinion.

C. Television's need for images creates a temptation to escalate ongoing action for the cameras or even to stage action that would not otherwise take place. Vigilance is necessary to avoid coverage that might lead to charges of misrepresentation, sensationalism, and deception.

D. Many news items are actually pseudoevents—contrived happenings created specifically to attract media coverage. Press conferences, photo opportunities, and "not-for-attribution" news briefings are all pseudoevents.

E. Publicity crimes committed by terrorist groups are a paradoxical blend of pseudoevents and real events. These bombings, hijackings, and kidnappings create ethical dilemmas for the news media.

F. Radio and television coverage of judicial processes, once banned, is now allowed in many courtrooms. Various "sunshine laws" and the Freedom of Information Act have given journalists greater access to the activities of governmental bodies and the files of government agencies.

15.5 Consequences for Political Life

A. The electronic media can allay panic and ease stress during crisis situations. Two examples were the assassination of President John Kennedy in 1963 and the House Judiciary Committee hearings on impeachment charges against Richard Nixon in 1974.

B. First radio and later television have had a powerful influence upon the conduct of political campaigns. Most political television spots are the products of advertising agencies. Party conventions are staged to accommodate television, and televised debates between major party candidates are now a factor in many elections (Exhibit 15.2).

C. Virtually any action an American president takes has inherent news value. Extensive media coverage goes automatically to whomever holds this office, giving the incumbent a tremendous advantage over political opponents.

D. A president who chooses to address the American people may request, and is almost always given, simultaneous coverage on all three television networks (Exhibit 15.3).

E. Although House and Senate committee hearings have been broadcast since the 1950s, Congress has been slow to allow coverage of its general sessions. In 1979 the House of Representatives established its own closed-circuit television system. Commercial broadcasters use only occasional excerpts, but gavel-to-gavel coverage is carried on the C-SPAN cable network. The Senate inaugurated a similar television operation in 1986 (Exhibit 15.4).

F. Television coverage of the Vietnam conflict provided the American public with its first "living room war" (Exhibit 15.5). Initial coverage presented a "sanitized" version of the war that stressed U.S. efficiency and might. Later coverage gave TV viewers a very different view that led eventually to American disillusionment.

G. During the 1984 invasion of Grenada, military authorities enforced a tight news blackout for the first two days of the operation. Since then, the Department of Defense has established a news-pool arrangement to allow for coverage of future military actions.

15.6 Entertainment

A. Critics note that some television dramas contain stock characters who perpetuate racial, sexual, and ethnic stereotypes. They also note that the world of television fiction contains an unrealistically higher proportion of detectives, scientists, business executives, and adventurers than the real world. Further, fictional characters are much more likely to resolve problems with decisive, highly visible acts that often involve violence.

B. Broadcasting has become a major agent of socialization for children. Researchers believe that certain programs (*Sesame Street*, *Fat Albert*) have prosocial effects while other programs (action/adventure programs with a high violence content) have antisocial effects.

C. Critics fault the public for giving so much time to the passive absorption of radio and television. But no one has demonstrated that listening and watching necessarily displace more useful and active forms of recreation.

15.7 Impact of Violence

A. Some individuals believe that televised violence has a direct effect and can cause at least some viewers to imitate the violent behavior they see on television. Research has demonstrated that TV (or film) viewing is, at most, a contributing factor. TV viewing is but one item in a string of events and characteristics that taken together may, in some circumstances, lead to antisocial behavior.

B. More concern is focused on the possible generalized effects of mediated violence on at least some individuals. A 1972 statement by the U.S. Surgeon General said "...the causal relationship between televised violence and antisocial behavior is sufficient to warrant appropriate and immediate remedial action." Because of First Amendment concerns and the trend to deregulation, no governmental action has occurred.

C. Beginning with the 1967-68 television season, George Gerbner and his associates at the University of Pennsylvania have conducted an annual analysis of the level of violence in programming. (Gerbner's content analysis is controversial, in part because he uses a coding system that includes violent acts found in animated cartoons.) Gerbner believes that violence in programs creates anxiety in viewers because they perceive the real world in terms of the television world (Exhibit 15.6).

D. Gerbner's hypothesis reverses an older hypothesis that predicts that people exposed to fictional violence will become *desensitized* to real-life violence. A related hypothesis holds that viewers become indifferent to violence because it is depicted so unrealistically (*sanitized*) on television.

E. Defenders of current practice argue that violence in television merely reflects violence in real life. To pretend that it doesn't exist would restrict writers unreasonably. The *catharsis* theory provides another justification of violent content. This concept hypothesizes that aggressive tendencies in television viewers will be drained away in harmless fantasies as a result of watching fictional TV violence. Most experimental studies, however, do not support this assumption.

KEY TERMS AND NAMES

A. *Research and methodology*

1. No single explanation or ______________________ has emerged to describe the impact media have on individuals and society.

2. Instead, researchers have examined the ______________________ of communicating and have developed ______________________ that identify the various elements involved as well as diagraming their interrelationships.

3. The ______________________ model implies that media content has a direct causal relationship on behavior.

4. The ______________________ model puts more emphasis on process than on content. It also stresses what individuals do with the media rather than what the media do to audiences.

5. The ______________________ model sees the media as but one of many factors that interact to bring about specific behavioral outcomes.

6. Media-effects data consist primarily of ______________________ responses that are beyond the reach of direct observation or measurement.

7. Opinion polls and audience rating reports are two examples of ________________. These techniques are used to gather data in natural settings.

8. ______________________ examines and summarizes the content of communication materials.

9. ______________________ enable investigators to control various experimental factors and to obtain both subjectively reported and objectively observed data.

10. Research efforts that attempt to observe behavior in real-world situations are called ______________________.

11. Research efforts that attempt to control extraneous influences while, at the same time, observing behavior in real-world situations are called ______________________.

B. *Advertising and news*

1. Advertising, claims economist John Kenneth Galbraith, is a ______________________ that stimulates demand for unneeded goods and services.

2. Many advertisements are created to retain the brand ______________________ of current product users while changing the purchasing habits of those who buy competitive products.

3. Those individuals who both select and position the items in a newscast are called

_______________________________.

4. The longer-term process of selecting and ranking issues determines the direction of public opinion. This process is called _______________________________.

5. When the media select a person or event for news coverage, they automatically confer a degree of _______________________________ on the person or event.

6. The very presence of television cameras sometimes results in the _______________________ of events that might not otherwise have occurred.

7. Contrived happenings that are scheduled specifically to attract media coverage are called

_______________________________.

8. Business and government public relations departments sometimes supply _______________________________ to television stations who may choose to include them in newscasts.

9. News media face an ethical dilemma when they determine what, if any, coverage to give _______________________________ committed by terrorist organizations.

10. Various _______________________________ have been enacted that require governmental agencies to meet in public where their actions can be observed and reported by the media.

11. The _______________________________ Act gives both individuals and the news media access to many types of government information previously withheld from public scrutiny.

C. *Politics, entertainment, and violence*

1. White House staffs frequently gain media coverage for incumbent presidents by scheduling _______________________________ during which the president can be seen greeting a visitor or performing a ceremonial function.

2. *New Yorker* television critic Michael Arlen has used the term ________________ to describe the impact of television's coverage of the Vietnam conflict on the American public.

3. Critics note that much of TV's early coverage of fighting in Vietnam as well as much of the fictional violence in televised drama is ________________ to make it less objectionable to viewers.

4. The Italian gangster, the mad scientist, and the bespectacled librarian are oversimplified characterizations or ________________ that perpetuate certain preconceived images already held by many viewers.

5. The lifelong process that teaches a child the rules of behavior as well as the value system of that child's culture is called ________________.

6. Content analysis has been used by ________________ and his associates to construct a "violence profile" for each television season since 1967–68.

7. One hypothesis predicts that people who are routinely exposed to fictional violence become ________________ or indifferent to real-life violence.

8. Another hypothesis suggests that viewers who watch fictional violence will experience a ________________ that defuses aggressive tendencies.

SELF-TEST

Fill in the Blank

1. Most audience research conducted during the 1930 to 1950 period focused on the effects of which media? ________________ and ________________

2. Most audience research since 1950 has concentrated on which medium?

____

3. Various ______________________ have been developed to diagram the steps in the process of communication.

4. ______________________ is a tool that allows researchers to categorize and quantify the material contained in television programs, movies, and other media forms.

5. Television's visual bias creates an involuntary ______________________ that gives news coverage to certain events while denying coverage to other events.

6. Which president used radio extensively to by-pass unfriendly newspapers and appeal directly to the voters? ______________________

7. The first president to use television commercials during a political campaign was ______________________. The first presidential candidates to debate on television were ______________________ and ______________________.

8. For fourteen years, from 1961 to 1975, network television gave extensive coverage to the war in ______________________. Military censorship prevented news coverage during the 1984 invasion of ______________________.

9. Some television programs have been designed to achieve positive or ______________________ effects among viewers. Other programs may inadvertently stimulate negative or ______________________ effects.

10. Five volumes of reports and papers dealing with the effects of ______________________ on human behavior were summarized by the U.S. Surgeon General during a 1972 Senate committee hearing.

True/False

T F 1. No single theory of mass communication explains the impact the mass media have on individuals and society.

T F 2. Joseph Klapper's 1960 book gave scientific sanction to the "law of minimal effects."

T F 3. One strength of the uses-and-gratifications model is the emphasis it gives to entertainment as a major element in media content.

T F 4. Laboratory experiments are less intrusive than field studies.

T F 5. In content analysis, the researcher selects and defines the content categories to be quantified.

T F 6. Field experiments are used more frequently than either laboratory experiments or field studies.

T F 7. The authors suggest that advertising is a more equitable way of charging the public for a broadcast service than the set-use license fee widely used in other countries.

T F 8. Children as young as three years are able to recognize the purpose of advertising and distinguish between commercials and program content.

T F 9. Agenda setting might be defined as long-term gatekeeping.

T F 10. The very presence of well-known anchors and correspondents confers importance to the stories they cover.

T F 11. After investigating charges that all three networks staged fake news stories during the 1968 Democratic convention, the FCC condemned the practice, fined each network $10,000, and issued guidelines to ensure that similar activities would not be repeated.

T F 12. All three television networks, as a matter of policy, will not give coverage to terrorist groups that engage in publicity crimes.

T F 13. Bona fide news and public-affairs programs about political candidates have less credibility with voters than do political advertising spots and candidate-controlled appearances.

T F 14. Network reporting of voting trends on election day is of particular concern to congressmen from West Coast states.

T F 15. All three networks are required by the Communications Act of 1934 to make time available to a president who wishes to address the American people about a matter of national concern.

T F 16. The actual television coverage of House and Senate debates is a shared responsibility of ABC, CBS, NBC, and the Cable News Network.

T F 17. Television coverage of the Vietnam conflict was tightly controlled and heavily censored by the military.

T F 18. Broadcasting has come to play an increasing role in the socialization process.

T F 19. The five-volume report of the Surgeon General's Advisory Committee on Television and Social Behavior has brought about a significant change in the nature and quantity of televised violence.

T F 20. Sociologists note that there is a lower level of social violence in Japan than in the United States. They relate this to the lower level of violence found in Japanese television dramas.

PROJECT

Select three dramatic television programs that contain violence as an integral part of the story line. View at least one of the programs to determine what kinds of content can be quantified. Then develop categories and perform a content analysis for each program. Your categories might include the following: (1) number of criminal acts committed, (2) occurrences of verbal abuse by "villains," (3) occurrences of verbal abuse by "heroes," (4) physical acts that inflict bodily injury on "heroes," (5) physical acts that inflict bodily injury on "villains," (6) physical acts that result in death to "heroes," (7) physical acts that result in death to "villains," (8) chase scenes (9) automobile crashes, and (10) arrests made by police officers. Use the results of your analysis to determine which of the three programs are the most and the least violent.

PART 6

Controls

CHAPTER 16

Agencies of Control

CHAPTER FOCUS

Broadcasters and cable operators are subject to laws imposed by Congress as well as regulations enacted by the Federal Communications Commission. Broadcast stations are licensed by the FCC to serve in "the public interest, convenience, and necessity." Although the FCC is the principal agency involved in the control of communications, other agencies and groups exercise authority in certain areas. Some of the controls are informal and come from citizen groups, industry codes, and professional self-regulation.

CAPSULE

Main points from each section of Chapter 16 are summarized below.

16.1 Constitutional Context

A. Government intrusion in any form of communication would ordinarily be prohibited by the First Amendment. However, some regulation of broadcasting is necessary to prevent interference and ensure that the scarce radio and television channels are utilized in ways that serve the public interest.

B. Congress and the courts have relied on this *scarcity factor* as a major justification for government regulation throughout the evolution of broadcast law. Opponents of traditional regulation dismiss the scarcity factor as outdated. They cite an increase in the number of stations now broadcasting as well as the availability of cable channels.

C. Broadcasting has been interpreted to be a form of interstate commerce and, under the terms of the commerce clause in the Constitution, is subject to the jurisdiction of Congress. When Congress passed the Communications Act of 1934, it created the Federal Communications Commission to act on its behalf (Exhibit 16.1).

D. FCC rules and regulations carry the force of federal law. The FCC has discretionary power, but its rules and decisions may be appealed to—and are sometimes reversed by—federal courts.

16.2 Communications Act Basics

A. Broadcasting provisions from the Radio Act of 1927 were reenacted in Title III of the Communications Act of 1934. Additional provisions were added to give the Federal Communications Commission control of interstate and foreign wire communication. The act contains seven major divisions or *titles.*

B. The act distinguishes between *broadcasting* and *common carrier.* Telephone companies and other common carriers supply communication services on a nondiscriminatory basis and without regard to content. Rates charged by common carriers are usually subject to government approval.

C. Broadcasting is defined as "the dissemination of radio communications *intended to be received by the public.*" Rates may be set by individual stations and networks and are *not* subject to approval by any government agency. Broadcasters, unlike common carriers, determine and retain responsibility for the content of the messages they transmit.

D. Cable television is neither a common carrier nor a broadcaster. The FCC has some responsibilities for cable, but they are far less extensive than its responsibilities for either broadcasting or interstate wire systems.

E. The FCC has five members who are appointed by the president and confirmed by the Senate. No more than three of the five commissioners may be of the same political party.

F. The words "public interest, convenience, and necessity" appear frequently in various places in the Communications Act of 1934. Congress used this deliberately vague phrase because it wanted to give the FCC maximum flexibility to evaluate unforeseeable situations and use its own judgment in making regulatory decisions.

16.3 Communications Act Issues

A. Although the Communications Act of 1934 has been amended many times since its enactment, the underlying philosophy of the act remains the same. The largest single amendment occurred in 1984 with the passage of the Cable Communications Policy Act and its inclusion into the 1934 act as Title VI.

B. A critic of the act, broadcast historian Erik Barnouw, wrote that both the 1927 and 1934 acts were based on the false premise that "broadcasting was a local responsibility exercised by independent station licensees." In reality, the vast majority of programs come from the networks and from other national syndication sources.

C. Several attempts to replace the 1934 act were introduced during the 1978–81 period. Some of the issues addressed included a redefinition of the public-interest standard, a proposal for spectrum-usage fees, and lengthening of the station license from three years to an indefinite period.

D. Only one of these proposals was formalized into law—the extension of the station license. In 1981 Congress changed the length of licenses for radio stations from three to seven years; licenses for television stations were extended from three to five years.

16.4 Telecommunication Policy

A. Broadcasting and cable television must be considered in the larger context of telecommunication policy. The Office of Telecommunications Policy was created in 1970 to examine long-range concerns, as opposed to the day-to-day operational focus of the FCC. It was replaced in 1978 by a new agency, the National Telecommunications and Information Administration (NTIA).

B. The Communications Act of 1934 gives the president responsibility for federal government agency users of the electromagnetic spectrum. This role is delegated to the NTIA. The FCC's responsibility is limited to the regulation of state and local government users of the spectrum as well as private users such as commercial and noncommercial broadcasters (Exhibit 16.2).

C. A special coordinating body, the Interdepartmental Radio Advisory Committee (IRAC), includes representatives from all federal agencies using the spectrum. NTIA supplies the chairperson and the administrative support for IRAC and represents the executive branch. The FCC is a member of IRAC, where it represents Congress and acts as liaison for nonfederal and private users.

D. A political trend, backed by economic evidence, has been to allow the marketplace rather than government to determine the direction of telecommunications policy. The result since the mid-1970s has been a relaxing of government regulation and greater emphasis on competition and marketplace pressures. Cable television has already been substantially deregulated. Some deregulation of radio and television has begun and further deregulation appears likely.

16.5 Copyright

A. Authors and musicians retain ownership of their creative works under terms of the Copyright Act of 1976. Copyright holders may license others to use their works in exchange for payment of royalties. "Use" consists of publishing, performing, displaying, and related activities.

B. A copyright is good for the life of the author plus 50 more years. Upon expiration, the work passes into the public domain and can be used without securing permission or paying a royalty.

C. Owners of copyrighted material who license television stations to use their works must grant *retransmission rights* to cable systems who pick up such programs and deliver them to subscribers (Exhibit 16.3).

D. The concept of *fair use* allows limited utilization of copyrighted materials for nonprofit educational use, criticism, and other limited purposes.

E. Radio and television stations pay music copyright fees to ASCAP, BMI, and SESAC. Most stations hold *blanket licenses* with ASCAP and BMI that allow the stations to use any music in the agencies' catalogs in return for an annual percentage of each station's gross income.

F. Television stations and networks have long objected to the blanket-licensing arrangement. TV uses much less music than radio, and the stations and networks would prefer to pay for individual works. Television broadcasters claim the blanket licenses are in violation of antitrust laws, but the Supreme Court has let stand an appeals court ruling that said otherwise.

G. The 1976 Copyright Act granted cable systems a compulsory license to retransmit copyrighted material broadcast on "distant-signal" stations such as Ted Turner's WTBS. In return for this license, cable systems must pay a fee to the Copyright Royalty Tribunal. This agency sets the fee and redistributes the proceeds to various copyright holders.

H. Receipt of cable television or of *scrambled* satellite programs without authorization and payment of required fees is *signal piracy.* The 1984 Cable Act makes such action illegal and provides both criminal and civil penalties for violators.

I. Another copyright issue involves the home recording of material from broadcast or cable sources and from rented cassettes. The Supreme Court has ruled that most recording of broadcast programs was for timeshifting purposes and did not constitute an infringement of copyright. However, the legality of recording cable or pay programming has not been resolved.

16.6 Other Laws Affecting Electronic Media

A. Program piracy can occur on an international basis. Satellite-distributed U.S. TV programs and cable entertainment channels are routinely pirated by Caribbean stations and cable systems. International copyright agreements are assuming increasing importance but are often difficult to enforce.

B. Press law relies heavily on common-law traditions and case-law precedents. Areas of concern include libel, obscenity, fair trial, freedom of access to information, right of privacy, antitrust laws, labor laws, advertising laws, copyright, and reporter's privileges. The last asserts the right of news personnel to withhold the identity of news sources and to refuse to surrender unpublished or unaired material.

C. The Federal Trade Commission (FTC), not the Federal Communications Commission, has authority to regulate broadcast advertising and protect consumers from unfair business practices including deceptive advertising.

D. Portions of the U.S. Criminal Code prohibit the broadcast of advertising or of information about lotteries. Congress has amended the law to permit station licensees to provide information and advertising for legalized state lotteries but only for those lotteries within their own or adjacent states. The U.S. Criminal Code also prohibits "obscene, indecent, or profane language."

E. The FCC has incorporated the federal equal-employment-opportunities (EEO) requirements within its own rules. Broadcast stations and cable systems are required to report the composition of their work forces in terms of sex and ethnic group (Exhibit 17.5).

F. Various state laws apply to the rights of individuals (libel), to advertising, to educational/public broadcasting, and to business operations. Some state and local regulations apply to cable television as well.

16.7 Informal Controls

A. Although Congress delegates authority to the FCC under the communications act, it also retains control over the agency in a number of ways. These begin with senatorial approval of the president's FCC nominees. Because Congress approves the commission's budget and conducts frequent hearings on its plans and performance, the FCC is extremely sensitive to congressional pressure and criticism. Broadcasters and cable operators lobby senators and representatives who often give a sympathetic view to their concerns.

B. Presidents sometimes use FCC commissioners to act as intermediaries between the White House and the broadcast industry. Presidents also make their views on regulatory issues known to the FCC. President Ronald Reagan held an "informational" talk with FCC Chairman Mark Fowler in 1984 and, shortly after, the commission abandoned its announced plans to drop the restrictions on network activity in program production and distribution.

C. Individual citizens and pressure groups also attempt to influence the behavior of broadcasters (Exhibit 16.4). Boycotts of advertised products are sometimes threatened by groups who object to programs or even proposed programs.

D. Consumer activism takes a more constructive and positive approach. One consumer-oriented interest has been in broadcast reform—especially concern for the quality of programming.

E. An important case involving WLBT, a Jackson, Mississippi, VHF station, gave legal precedent to the standing of consumer groups to challenge broadcasters before the FCC at license-renewal time. During the 1970s, many consumer groups filed such challenges. Some of these challenges were withdrawn after *negotiated settlements* were reached between the stations being challenged and the consumer groups.

F. In another case, a consumer group protested a format change proposed by Chicago radio Station WEFM. The FCC ruled in favor of the station and suggested that marketplace competition should be the only control over broadcast programming, a ruling upheld by the Supreme Court.

G. Consumerism has faced a hostile political climate in the 1980s and the number of active consumer groups at both the national and local levels has declined.

H. The National Association of Broadcasters (NAB) developed a voluntary code for radio programming and advertising practices in 1939 followed by a similar code for television in 1952. The codes established generally observed standards, particularly in the percentage of time given to advertising. The Department of Justice alleged that the codes deprived advertisers of "the benefits of free and open competition," and the NAB terminated the codes in 1982.

I. Program-standards departments at all three networks evaluate and sometimes edit commercials and programs. Cable television's standards are much less restrictive and this puts pressure on the networks to loosen their standards as well.

J. Some professional organizations have established codes of ethics. One such organization is the Radio and Television News Directors Association (RTNDA).

K. Writers in major newspapers and magazines offer programming criticism that has some impact. The most serious attempt at organized self-criticism, the National News Council, failed in 1984 after major newspapers refused to support the organization.

KEY TERMS

A. *Regulatory aspects*

1. In regulatory practices, broadcasting is treated differently from other forms of communication. Congress and the courts have used the ______________________ factor to justify this difference.

2. The word ______________________, initially used to describe the exchange of goods, can also be used to describe the exchange of information.

3. Major portions or chapters of federal law are referred to as ________________________.

4. Companies that supply communication services to anyone willing to pay a fixed price for those services are classified as ________________________.

5. ________________________ is defined as any form of radio communications intended to be received by the public.

6. The FCC is obligated to ensure that broadcast licensees operate in the ________________________, even though the phrase itself is subject to continuing interpretation.

7. A proposal to require commercial broadcasters to pay a ________________________ based on the economic value of each channel was vigorously opposed by the broadcasters and eventually dropped.

8. The agency within the Department of Commerce that acts as the president's adviser on telecommunications questions is the ________________________.

9. All federal agencies with a need for access to the electromagnetic spectrum send representatives to a special coordinating body known as the ________________________.

B. *Copyright*

1. The current legislation that grants authors and artists the right to protect and profit from their creative work is the ________________________.

2. Protection extends during the life of the author plus 50 additional years. After that the work enters the ________________________.

3. Owners of copyrighted materials who license television stations to use their works must grant ________________________ to cable systems that pick such programs off the air and deliver them to subscribers.

4. In certain limited circumstances, copyrighted materials may be used without securing permission under the concept of ________________________.

5. Stations who hold ______________________ from ASCAP and BMI pay a single fee to each agency and gain the right to use all of the music in each licensing agency's catalog.

6. The ______________________ established the rates paid by cable systems for use of copyrighted material. This same agency then has the responsibility to distribute the money collected among copyright holders.

7. Illegal cable hookups and unauthorized reception of scrambled television signals are two forms of ______________________.

C. *Other laws*

1. Audio and video materials excluded during the editing process from the final versions of news and documentary programs are called ______________________.

2. The Latin phrase ______________________ means "let the buyer beware."

3. In 1938 Congress rejected this doctrine and gave the ______________________ the responsibility to attack deceptive advertising.

4. In 1969 the FCC incorporated federal ______________________ requirements into its own rules in an attempt to eliminate discrimination in broadcasting.

D. *Information controls*

1. Citizen groups will sometimes attempt to influence the behavior of broadcasters by threatening to refuse to buy certain advertised products. This method of coercion is called a ______________________.

2. ______________________ is a media watchdog group that provides both criticism and even programs that offer a conservative reply to what the group believes is the liberal bias of networks and stations.

3. The long-term importance of the case involving ______________________, a Jackson, Mississippi, television station was the court decision directing the FCC to give ______________________ to citizen groups who wish to challenge existing licensees.

4. In 1971 the FCC required that stations keep license-renewal applications and other important documents in a ______________________ that is available to anyone seeking access to it.

5. During the 1970s various citizen groups filed petitions to deny the renewal of station licenses but often agreed to withdraw the petitions after agreeing to ______________________ with individual stations.

6. The ______________________ were voluntary guidelines that established program content and advertising time standards for member stations.

7. Members of the ______________________ subscribe to a "Code of Broadcast News Ethics" that obligates them to present news in a manner that serves the public interest.

8. From 1973 through 1984 the ______________________ made a serious attempt to provide organized self-criticism of the news media by conducting impartial investigations into complaints about news coverage.

SELF-TEST

Fill in the Blank

1. The ______________________ clause of the Constitution gives Congress the jurisdiction to regulate broadcasting.

2. FCC commissioners are appointed by the ______________________ and confirmed by the ______________________.

3. The legislation that created the FCC and governs various aspects of broadcasting as well as other forms of communication is the ______________________.

4. Telephone companies are classified as ______________________ whereas radio and television stations are classified as ______________________.

5. The current political trend suggests that ______________________ forces rather than government regulation should determine telecommunications policy.

6. Authors, composers, and other creative individuals can secure a ______________ to protect their creative products from unauthorized use.

7. The related concepts of compulsory licensing and of retransmission consent are of principal importance to ______________.

8. The Federal Trade Commission's involvement in broadcasting is focused primarily on ______________.

9. Although the FCC holds a great deal of discretionary power, there is a tendency for ______________ to second-guess it on most regulatory issues.

10. The FCC has ruled that radio stations are free to change their formats to meet the competition of the marketplace. Listener groups challenged this ruling. The issue went to the Supreme Court where the commission's decision was ______________.

11. The ______________ developed both a radio code and a television code that set voluntary standards within the industry until both codes were ended in 1982.

12. Cable television program standards are ______________ than those followed by broadcasters.

True/False

T F 1. Although the scarcity factor is under challenge, it still remains the principal justification for broadcast regulation.

T F 2. Telephone and telegraph services are subject to state rather than to federal jurisdiction.

T F 3. The Cable Communications Policy Act of 1984 became Title VI of the Communications Act of 1934.

T F 4. The prices broadcasters charge advertisers for commercial time are regulated by the FCC.

T F 5. Cable television has been classified as a broadcaster rather than as a common carrier.

T F 6. No more than three of the five FCC commissioners may be of the same political party.

T F 7. The phrase "public interest, convenience, and necessity" was initially applied to public utilities.

T F 8. Erik Barnouw believes that broadcast regulation is based on an invalid premise—the assumption that programming is a local responsibility exercised by independent station licensees.

T F 9. Both radio and television stations are granted licenses by the Federal Communications Commission for three-year periods.

T F 10. Questions of telecommunications policy are more properly under the jurisdiction of the NTIA than the FCC.

T F 11. The photocopying of a magazine article or the inclusion of a quotation in a paper or review, although frequently done, is nevertheless a violation of copyright.

T F 12. The Copyright Royalty Tribunal is both a collector and a distributor of payments from cable television.

T F 13. Individuals with satellite dishes are not obligated to obtain permission or pay a fee to receive and view unscrambled signals.

T F 14. While stations may use contests in promotional campaigns, they may not charge participants an entrance fee.

T F 15. Economic boycotts force advertisers to retreat from any involvement in program decision making.

T F 16. Although the consumerism movement began during an activist period in the 1960s, it was not until the 1980s that the movement gained strength and exerted any real influence on the broadcasting industry.

T F 17. Among practicing broadcasters, engineers and news personnel are the two groups that come closest to meeting the standards of professionalism.

T F 18. The failure of the National News Council can be attributed, in large part, to the unwillingness of major newspapers to support this organization.

PROJECT

Try to locate a copy of the former Television Code of the National Association of Broadcasters. Both the television and radio codes were printed in 1982 and earlier editions of *Broadcasting/Cablecasting Yearbook.* (Many libraries retain older yearbooks in their reference collections.) Note the contents of the code, particularly those portions that deal with advertising. Do you agree with the Department of Justice that the television code "artificially curtailed" advertising and repressed price competition?

As an alternative, contact a local radio or television station and request a copy of the broadcast and advertising standards in use at that station.

CHAPTER 17

FCC Administration of the Law

CHAPTER FOCUS

This chapter discusses the organization, structure, and role of the FCC and examines some of its procedures to license and regulate electronic media. The growing trend of deregulation, the Cable Communications Policy Act of 1984, and actions taken by the FCC to limit media monopolies and encourage diversity in media ownership are also examined.

CAPSULE

Main points from each section of Chapter 17 are summarized below.

17.1 FCC Basics

A. The Federal Communications Commission is one of many independent regulatory agencies created by Congress to supervise interstate commerce, power, transportation, and similar areas. The FCC performs *legislative functions* when it makes rules and regulations, *executive functions* when it orders certain actions, and *judicial functions* when it conducts hearings and decides disputes (Exhibit 17.1).

B. In fiscal year 1985, Congress appropriated $95 million for the operation of the FCC including salary for its staff of 1,900.

C. The five commissioners are appointed by the president and confirmed by the Senate. They serve five-year terms and may be reappointed. Many serve only a few years, however, before resigning to enter or resume private law practice. (Most commissioners are lawyers by profession.)

D. Much of the work of the FCC is handled by professional staff and does not come to the personal attention of the commissioners. With few exceptions, staff members are part of the federal civil service.

E. Prior to issuing a formal rule, the commission issues either a *notice of inquiry* or a *notice of proposed rule making.* These notices invite comment from interested parties. After digesting these comments, the staff prepares a decision in the form of a *report and order* for consideration by the commissioners. FCC decisions are subject to petition for reconsideration and appeal to the U.S. Court of Appeals for the District of Columbia.

F. In some situations, the FCC issues a statement of general policy rather than a more specific formal rule.

G. Disputes between opposing parties are settled through a detailed process of adjudication (Exhibit 17.2).

H. The FCC influences industry conduct through informal regulation. Speeches and articles are examples of a raised-eyebrow approach and direct contact is called jawboning.

17.2 Deregulation

A. The current deregulatory trend began in the 1970s during the administrations of Gerald Ford and Jimmy Carter, and accelerated under Ronald Reagan (Exhibit 17.3).

B. In 1981 the FCC removed four obligations previously required of radio stations. These included ascertainment of community needs, the keeping of program logs, the minimum guidelines for nonentertainment programming, and the guidelines for setting a maximum level of advertising time.

C. Ascertainment and logging requirements were lifted in 1984 for noncommercial radio and television stations and for commercial television stations. Programming and advertising guidelines were lifted for the latter as well.

D. Television networks were the subject of the FCC's third intensive inquiry. The staff report of 1980 concluded that prior network regulation had not increased diversity of programming but had instead protected networks from the competition of new technologies. The report recommended and the commissioners considered deleting both the Prime-Time Access Rule (PTAR) and two rules restricting network ownership and distribution of off-network programs. Pressure from Congress and from the president prevented the commission from implementing these deregulatory changes.

E. The FCC has all but stopped oversight of cable television. The commission's must-carry rule required cable systems to carry the signals of local television stations. This rule was unpopular with cable systems, especially those with a limited number of channels, because it reduced the number of channels available for cable-specific programs. The rule was overturned in federal court as a violation of cable operators' First Amendment rights. Cable operators can pick and choose among TV stations in filling their channels.

F. The FCC has also reexamined its role as a setter of technology regulations. The commission decided not to choose among five competing AM stereo systems in 1982. It decided instead to allow AM stations to use any one of the five, thereby leaving the eventual choice of systems to the marketplace. Similar decisions have been made with regard to DBS, teletext, television stereo, and other services.

17.3 Licensing

A. Radio and television stations are licensed to use portions of the electromagnetic spectrum for five years (for television) or seven years (for radio). Users may not claim ownership of a channel or a right to broadcast beyond those terms specifically imposed by the license.

B. Would-be licensees for FM and TV channels must consult FCC allotment tables to determine if channels are available in their communities. Applicants for AM channels must employ engineering consultants to determine if an AM channel can be activated without causing interference to existing stations.

C. In most markets, all desirable channels have long since been taken. Thus, would-be licensees nearly always seek to buy an existing station.

D. Operators of new stations must first apply for a construction permit or CP. The CP holder then has a limited time (usually 18 months) to put a test signal on the air and satisfy a proof-of-performance requirement. If the testing is satisfactory, the applicant may then apply for a full license.

E. The Communications Act specifies that licenses can be granted only to U.S. citizens who qualify as to *character*, *financial ability*, and *technical ability*. As applicants competing for a license usually meet these minimum requirements, the FCC often considers other qualifications such as local ownership or the role of minorities in station management.

F. When several would-be licensees apply for the same channel in the same market, they are called *mutually exclusive* applicants. The FCC makes a choice among them after conducting *comparative hearings* which can be lengthy and costly proceedings.

G. Congress authorized the FCC to use a lottery system of random selection to choose among the huge pool of qualified applicants for new, low-power television (LPTV) licenses. Similar procedures were established for a variety of nonmedia licenses such as cellular telephone systems and Multichannel Multipoint Distribution Systems (MMDS). The commission made it clear that lotteries would not be used to award licenses for regular broadcasting services.

H. Cable licensing is not the responsibility of the FCC. Cable franchises are awarded by municipal governments.

17.4 Operating under License

A. The responsibility of a licensee to maintain control over a station's operation is *non-delegable.* Licensees retain responsibility for all content even if possibly offensive material is in a foreign language or within the lyrics of rock music.

B. Equal Employment Opportunities (EEO) requirements apply to applicants and existing licensees. The commission has established guidelines that reflect employment patterns within a licensee's market area (Exhibit 17.4).

C. Each station is required to maintain a *public file* and make that file available during normal business hours to anyone on request.

D. Most stations keep one or more Washington-based lawyers with communications expertise on retainer. These lawyers monitor the activities of the FCC and keep their clients properly informed.

E. The commission maintains a Complaints and Investigations Branch within its Mass Media Bureau to review and respond to letters and petitions from the public.

17.5 License Renewal

A. Although more than 98 percent of all licenses are renewed, broadcasters still fear a process that might remove their right to operate and put them off the air and out of business.

B. The communications act requires that licenses shall be renewed if the "public interest, convenience, and necessity" would be served by renewal. In making a decision, the FCC can use any information accumulated in the licensee's file during the license period.
C. In 1981, as part of deregulation, the FCC adopted a simple post card renewal form (Exhibit 17.5). Five percent of renewal applicants, picked at random, must fill out a more complicated "audit" form similar to the renewal form used for all licensees prior to 1981.
D. Some 99 percent of all renewal applications are uncontested and FCC staff members have the delegated authority to renew these licenses automatically.
E. A *petition to deny* renewal may come from a citizen group that opposes an incumbent licensee because the group believes the incumbent has failed to meet public-interest standards. *Mutually exclusive applications* may come from would-be licensees trying to displace an incumbent and claiming that they can do a better job of serving the public interest (Exhibit 17.6).
F. In deciding between incumbents and competing applicants, the FCC faces the dilemma of comparing an *actual* past service with a *proposed* future service. The tendency is to favor the incumbent.
G. Cable franchises are renewed by the local franchising authority, not the FCC.

17.6 The Cable Policy Act

A. The FCC and the courts, using language from the 1934 Communications Act, improvised control of cable television until passage of the Cable Communications Policy Act of 1984. This amendment to the 1934 act codified a strong deregulatory approach to cable.
B. The 1984 Act defined cable as a one-way video programming medium; two-way services are not included. Public, educational, and government ("PEG") access channels may be required by local franchising authorities. These authorities may charge a franchise fee of no more than 5 percent of gross cable revenues (and most do).
C. Cable systems with more than 36 channels must set aside 10 to 15 percent of their channels for *leased access.* Cable companies are barred from ownership of overlapping television stations or telephone companies (except in rural areas for the latter).
D. Rates for basic cable service may not be regulated by federal or state agencies. Local agencies may regulate rates but only in certain circumstances. Rates for pay cable services are not subject to regulation by any governmental authority. Signal piracy is subject to fines and imprisonment.
E. The FCC's equal-employment-opportunity reporting guidelines apply to cable systems.
F. Local authorities regulate cable under terms of a franchise that usually runs for 10 to 15 years. This franchise specifies the quality of service to be provided, technical standards, and the franchise fee to be paid.
G. A franchise is awarded in a competitive process. Interested companies respond to a *request for proposals (RFP)* issued by the franchise authority and submit bids that are then evaluated by that authority.

17.7 Mass Media Ownership Regulation

A. Unregulated competition can produce media monopoly. Such monopoly can lead to a reduction in the level or diversity of information, ideas, and opinions within a marketplace. Diversification of media ownership and control has been a goal of FCC regulation.

B. The 12-12-12 rule limits single owners (including networks) to no more than 12 stations in each service (AM-FM-TV). For television stations, the total potential audience may not exceed 25 percent of the nation's television households.
C. The *duopoly* rule limits single owners to one station of each kind in the same market.
D. The "one-to-a-customer" rule prohibits ownership of radio-television combinations in the same market. Those holding combinations prior to enactment of the rule in 1970 were *grandfathered* and allowed to retain both radio and television properties. Should those combinations be sold, however, the radio and television stations must go to separate owners.
E. There is no limit on multiple ownership of cable systems or LPTV. And noncommercial stations are exempt from both the duopoly and the one-to-a-customer rules.
F. In 1975 the FCC issued rules banning ownership of newspapers and broadcasting stations within the same market. All but a few existing combinations were grandfathered.
G. Broadcast networks may not own cable systems. As noted earlier, local television stations may not own cable systems that fall in their primary coverage area. Nor may telephone companies operate cable companies in their service area.
H. The FCC has adopted two policies intended to enhance the opportunities for members of minority groups to become licensees. One policy grants *tax certificates* that permit deferral of capital gains to licensees proposing to sell stations to minority interests. The second permits a *distress sale* whereby an owner of a license under threat of nonrenewal may sell the station for 75 percent of its appraised value to minority interests. In 1982 the FCC expanded both doctrines by allowing their use when an ethnic minority held as little as 20 percent of license equity but had a strong voice in management.

17.8 Enforcement

A. The most severe penalty the FCC can impose on a station is loss of license. Less severe penalties include fines and short-term licenses.
B. Loss of license cannot be imposed without lengthy hearings and appeals procedures. Appeals of an FCC decision involving station licenses must go to the Court of Appeals for the District of Columbia Circuit. Appeals of FCC decisions not involving licenses may be initiated in any of the eleven other U.S. courts of appeal.
C. From 1934 through 1984, only 149 stations have lost their licenses and almost all of these were due to nonrenewal rather than revocation, the canceling of a license before its normal term expires. In revocation hearings, the burden of proof is on the FCC to demonstrate that continuing use of the license is not in the public interest. In renewal hearings, the burden of proof is on the station to demonstrate that the public interest would be served by such renewal (Exhibit 17.7).
D. Nonrenewals have occurred for various reasons including fraudulent billing, character defects of the licensee, staging of news, violation of technical rules, and misrepresentation.
E. Short-term renewals (usually for a year rather than the usual term) put the licensee on probation, pending the correction of deficiencies. Conditional renewals may be granted, pending correction of some specific fault.
F. Forfeitures (fines) may range from as little as $25 to a maximum of $20,000. Most fines are imposed for violations of technical operating rules.

17.9 FCC Issues

A. There has been recurring criticism of the appointment process used to select members of the Federal Communications Commission.

B. Constant interaction between commissioners and the people they regulate creates suspicion of ex parte contacts. Commission meetings are now open to the public.

C. FCC chairman Mark Fowler has stated repeatedly that broadcasting should be governed by market forces rather than by agency supervision. He has transformed the commission into a more efficient processor of applications on the one hand and an active deregulator on the other.

KEY TERMS

A. *FCC basics*

1. The Federal Communications Commission is but one of a series of ________________ established by Congress to supervise federal involvement in commerce, power, transportation, and similar areas.

2. One duty of the FCC is to test electronic devices to ensure that they will not cause interference with other services. The FCC laboratory grants ________________ to those devices that pass this test.

3. When the FCC is considering a particular action, it will invite comment from interested parties by issuing either a ________________ or a ________________.

4. The legal document that announces an FCC rule and provides some background discussion is called a ________________.

5. In some situations, the FCC may prefer to issue a statement of general ________________ rather than a restrictive rule.

6. The term ________________ is used to describe the FCC's procedures for settling disputes between outside parties or between units within the commission.

7. FCC commissioners will sometimes make an implied threat of regulation in a formal statement or publication. Such statements are actually a type of informal regulation known as the ________________ approach.

8. A more intense kind of informal regulation involves frank discussions and a certain amount of pressure on industry leaders. These discussions are referred to as

   ______________________________.

9. The networks and the National Association of Broadcasters voluntarily adopted

   ______________________________ standards of program content although a district court judge held that the policy violated the First Amendment.

10. Broadcasters will sometimes air an ______________________________ before a program to warn viewers that program content may not be appropriate for a general-family audience.

11. Under deregulation, the FCC has deleted the requirement that stations engage in a formal

    process of ______________________________ to determine local community problems.

12. Also eliminated was the requirement that stations keep specifically formatted

    ______________________________ to indicate what they had aired during a given period.

B. *Licensing*

1. Would-be licensees must first apply for a ______________________________. This document enables them to conduct "proof-of-performance" testing that must be satisfactory before a license can be granted.

2. Two or more competitors for the same license are called ______________________________ applicants. The FCC makes a choice among them after conducting

   ______________________________.

3. The FCC does not license cable systems. Instead, municipal jurisdictions grant a type of

   license known as ______________________________.

4. Station licensees have a ______________________________ to maintain control over a station's operation and especially its programming.

5. The FCC requires that every station maintain certain documents in a

   ______________________________ that individuals may examine during business hours.

6. Most lawyers who represent stations in FCC dealings belong to the

_______________________________.

7. Most applications for license renewal are _______________________________ and FCC staff members have the delegated authority to grant these renewals automatically.

8. Citizen groups that believe incumbent licensees have failed to meet public-interest standards may file a _______________________________ in an attempt to influence the FCC's decision-making process and prevent renewal.

9. Those senior staff members at the FCC who conduct hearings and make rulings in license disputes hold the title of _______________________________.

C. *Cable*

1. The trade group that represents cable operators and was instrumental in protecting their interests during discussions leading to the Cable Communications Policy Act of 1984 is the _______________________________.

2. Two groups that represented the interests of municipal governments during these discussions were _______________________________ and _______________________________.

3. Cable systems may be required by local authorities to provide three access channels known collectively as _______________________________ channels.

4. Cable systems with more than 36 channels must set aside 10 to 15 percent of those channels for _______________________________ usage.

5. The 1984 cable act gives local franchise authorities the option to charge cable systems a _______________________________ of no more than 5 percent of gross cable revenues.

6. Franchise authorities invite bids from prospective cable companies by issuing a _______________________________ that stipulates the proposed system design, anticipated services, and timetable desired by the community.

D. *Ownership, enforcement, and issues*

1. Individuals or corporations that hold newspapers as well as radio or television stations are engaged in ______________________________ ownership.

2. The FCC's ______________________________ rule limits single owners to more than ______________________________ stations in each service–AM, FM, and TV.

3. The ______________________________ rule prohibits a single owner from having more than one station of each kind in a given market.

4. Ownership of AM-FM-TV combinations is prohibited by a 1975 FCC ruling, yet many of these combinations exist because of a ______________________________ provision exempting those who held the stations at the time of the ruling.

5. Licensees who sell stations to minority interests receive an incentive from the FCC in the form of ______________________________ that allow the former owners to defer capital-gains taxes if they purchase another station within two years.

6. The FCC has also agreed to allow the ______________________________ of stations under threat of nonrenewal if the owner is willing to sell the property to a minority group for 75 percent of its appraised value.

7. Lengthy court battles are sometimes avoided when parties accused of illegal practices sign ______________________________ agreeing to stop the alleged practices although not admitting guilt.

8. The ______________________________ clause of the Fifth Amendment guarantees parties the right to present their cases for adjudication under nondiscriminatory conditions. It also guarantees the right of appeal.

9. Before imposing a fine on a licensee, the FCC is required to invite the licensee to ______________________________ why such action should not be taken.

10. To which court must any appeal of an FCC action concerning a station license be taken?

____

11. The court may confirm or overturn commission actions. It may also _______________ a case back to the commission for further consideration.

12. Court decisions may be appealed to the Supreme Court. The request for consideration by the Supreme Court is called a _______________.

13. When the FCC cancels a license before its normal term expires, a process called _______________, the commission must prove that the public interest would best be served by such action.

14. When the FCC grants a _______________, it puts the licensee on probation pending the correction of general deficiencies evident during the previous license period.

15. The FCC may grant a _______________, pending correction of some specific fault.

16. Penalties for day-to-day infractions of the rules take the form of fines or _______________ that may range from $25 to $20,000.

17. Private meetings between commissioners and representatives of the industries they regulate are unethical and, in some cases, illegal. Such meetings are referred to as _______________ contacts.

18. The FCC chairman appointed by Ronald Reagan who believes that broadcasting should be governed by market forces rather than by traditional regulatory practices is _______________.

SELF-TEST

Fill in the Blank

1. In 1982 the number of FCC commissioners was reduced from seven to _______________.

2. Although all commissioners are political appointees, all but a very few members of the staff are members of the federal ______________.

3. While deregulation is usually welcomed by the broadcasting industry, this is not always the case. For example, program syndicators successfully lobbied to prevent the FCC from dropping the ______________ Rule.

4. The most controversial FCC restriction on cable was the ______________ rule that required cable systems to include the signals of certain television stations in their basic service.

5. Section 308 of the communications act stipulates that licenses be granted only to U.S. citizens who qualify as to ______________, ______________, and ______________.

6. Most regulation of cable television is done not by the FCC but rather at the ______________ level of government.

7. Stations with five or more fulltime employees must file an ______________ plan with the FCC and also submit Form 395 annually.

8. Since 1981 the FCC has adopted a license-renewal form that consists of a ______________.

9. When deciding between an incumbent broadcaster and a competing applicant, the FCC is left with the dilemma of comparing ______________ with ______________.

10. The term of most cable franchises varies from ______________ to ______________ years.

11. No single owner may own more than ______________ television stations; nor may the potential audience for those TV stations exceed ______________ percent of television households in the United States.

12. In license-renewal hearings, the burden of proof as to whether the public interest will be served is on the ______________________________. In revocation hearings, the burden of proof is on the ______________________________.

13. Two penalties the FCC can impose that are less severe than loss of the license include ______________________________ and ______________________________.

14. Most FCC commissioners are ______________________________ by profession.

True/False

T F 1. The Federal Communications Commission was the first of a series of independent regulatory agencies established by Congress.

T F 2. FCC commissioners meet as a decision-making group several times each month, in meetings open to the public.

T F 3. A "rule" differs from a "regulation" because a rule becomes effective immediately whereas a regulation does not take effect for sixty days.

T F 4. An FCC report and order is a final decision and cannot be challenged or appealed.

T F 5. The FCC has refused to establish a technical standard for AM stereo.

T F 6. An individual who wants to put a new AM station on the air in a specific community must first check the FCC allotment tables to see if any channels assigned to that community are vacant.

T F 7. A construction permit is a necessary step in the process of obtaining a station license.

T F 8. Congress has authorized the FCC to use a lottery system of random selection to award licenses to mutually exclusive applicants for radio and television channels.

T F 9. Although all stations are still required to maintain a public file, recent deregulatory decisions have reduced the amount of material kept in the file.

T F 10. Cable franchise fees are determined entirely by municipal authorities because the FCC no longer has any authority in this matter.

T F 11. While new AM-FM-TV combinations may not be created, existing combinations may be sold intact to a single owner.

T F 12. Networks may not own cable systems, although they may own cable programming services such as ESPN and Lifetime.

T F 13. Marginal radio stations that are struggling to survive are the ones that commit the greatest number of punishable rule infractions.

T F 14. FCC chairman Mark Fowler has suggested that television is simply a "toaster with pictures"and should be regulated like any other appliance.

T F 15. Those who support regulation by market forces favor structural rather than behavioral regulation of broadcasting.

PROJECT

Most major university libraries and all law libraries have a complete collection of *FCC Reports*, the official record of commission reports and orders. Select any one of the citations in this chapter. For example, the citation *78 FCC 2d 865, 1980* refers to a 1980 report and order that can be found on page 865 in volume 78 of the second series of reports.

Locate and read one or more of these documents. Then try to answer these questions. Who was involved and what was the issue? Did the order apply only to the one situation, or did it establish precedent for similar situations that might occur in the future? Was the decision by the commissioners unanimous? If not, did one or more of the commissioners file a dissenting opinion? Do you agree with the majority or minority viewpoint?

CHAPTER 18

Freedom and Fairness

CHAPTER FOCUS

The First Amendment protects freedom of speech and of the press. However, it applies somewhat differently to broadcasting and cable than to other media. Court decisions have supported the FCC's right to impose certain requirements on broadcasters to ensure that opposing viewpoints might be heard. Issues relating to the presentation of news and the presentation of politically oriented material are also discussed in this chapter.

CAPSULE

Main points from each section of Chapter 18 are summarized below.

18.1 First Amendment Basics

A. The purpose of the First Amendment is "to preserve an uninhibited marketplace of ideas in which truth will ultimately prevail." Conflicting ideas are encouraged.

B. The First Amendment specifically prohibits Congress from making any law abridging freedom of speech or of the press. Similarly, Section 326 of the Communications Act of 1934 specifically prohibits the FCC from engaging in censorship or interfering in the right of free speech by means of radio communication (see Box in text chapter).

C. A distinction must be made between government and private censorship. Although no government agency is permitted to restrict content, broadcast station and cable system officials may edit, revise, or delete program material without violating the First Amendment.

D. The courts have consistently held that broadcasting has a somewhat different First Amendment status than other media. Publishers have the right to print what they choose because they own the publishing facilities. Broadcasters cannot fully own their "publishing" facilities. They are temporary licensees, borrowing access to segments of the publicly owned electro-magnetic spectrum.

E. Although the broadcasting industry has argued that the FCC has the right to regulate only the technical aspects of broadcasting, the Supreme Court has ruled otherwise. The court has affirmed the commission's authority both to supervise traffic over the airwaves and to determine the composition of that traffic.

18.2 Unprotected Speech

A. Not all speech enjoys protection under the First Amendment. Speech, whether spoken or published, that falls into any of the following categories may be in violation of the law and subject to punishment: defamation, obscenity, plagiarism, invasion of privacy, or inciting an insurrection.

B. Even though these laws exist, they are administered with caution, because the threat of punishment might have a *chilling effect* on the willingness of journalists to present certain facts or ideas to the public (Exhibit 18.1).

C. In the 1964 case *New York Times v. Sullivan*, the Supreme Court ruled that criticism of public officials enjoys broad protection under the First Amendment. Litigants seeking damages must prove not only that a defamatory statement was false, but also that it was made with actual malice—that is, with knowledge that it was false or with reckless disregard of whether it was false or not. Later cases broadened the scope of this decision to include public figures as well as public officials.

D. In *Herbert v. Lando* (1979), the Supreme Court ruled that testimony could be taken and materials examined to determine the state of mind of reporters and editors who may be defendants in libel suits brought by public officials or public figures.

E. Invasion of privacy is closely related to libel. Both concepts fall under state rather than federal laws. There is an inherent conflict between an individual's right to privacy and the community's right to information of legitimate public interest. Again, those classified as public officials or public figures are accorded less protection under privacy laws than are ordinary citizens.

F. Current obscenity law is based on the 1973 case *Miller v. California.* The Supreme Court ruled that local courts should apply community standards when determining if material is obscene. Case law has established that questionable material cannot be judged in isolation but must be considered within the context of the entire work.

G. Obscenity in broadcasting is not well defined because only a few cases come to the attention of the FCC and fewer still are tested in court. In the WGLD-FM "topless radio" case, the FCC imposed a fine and urged the defendant to appeal. The station chose to pay the fine. However, in 1973 WBAI-FM, a station owned by Pacifica Radio, did appeal an FCC obscenity judgment on First Amendment grounds. The Supreme Court supported the FCC and noted that the questionable material, although not obscene, was indecent because it was broadcast during a time when children would normally be in the audience.

H. The 1984 cable act provides several penalties for those found guilty of transmitting obscene material over cable. Various state laws also regulate obscenity on cable. Still, the definition of obscene material is nebulous and will probably evolve through case law.

I. The Sixth Amendment right of an individual to receive a fair trial sometimes comes in conflict with the First Amendment right of the press to secure and report information. Intense publicity given to trials or pretrial proceedings may create an environment in which a fair trial becomes impossible. For several decades, there was virtually no radio, television, or film coverage or recording of trials. Now media equipment is less intrusive and the American Bar Association has recommended that judges be given wide latitude in allowing photo and video coverage of trials. Today, about half the states allow cameras in their courtrooms, but federal court restrictions against such coverage are still in effect (Exhibit 18.2).

18.3 Control over Programs

A. Although Section 326 prohibits the FCC from censoring programs, the commission is free to persuade and encourage the production of programs that meet the public-service criterion of the communications act. The commission specifically encourages the airing of locally produced programs that serve community needs.

B. The FCC's localism principle applies not only to what stations produce but also to the access these stations provide for individuals and groups within the community who want to air their points of view.

C. The continuing expansion of network and syndicated program revenue usually results in reduction in locally produced programs. FCC licensing and renewal policies still support localism as a goal, but the commission's localism concerns are more procedural than substantive in nature.

D. Broadcasters often cite the need to preserve localism when threatened by newer services such as cable and direct-broadcast satellite.

E. The most persistent advocates of localism and public-service programming are those that speak for children, minority groups, and the elderly. The issue is whether government can or should force a privately owned industry to produce certain types of programs. The recent trend of deregulation moves away from any kind of program controls.

18.4 Regulated Fairness

A. The FCC has sought to assure access to broadcasting for ideas rather than for specific people. The commission has developed a formalized set of procedures called the *fairness doctrine* to achieve this goal (Exhibit 18.3).

B. A 1941 FCC ruling, the "Mayflower" decision, stated that licensees took an unfair advantage when they used their facilities to express their own points of view in the form of editorials. A 1949 policy statement reversed that ruling and encouraged licensees to present controversial issues by means of editorials. It also required broadcasters to give outsiders access to express opposing points of view. Further, the commission held it was the "affirmative responsibility" of broadcasters to provide a reasonable amount of time for the discussion of public issues.

C. Two additional fairness requirements, the *personal attack rule* and the *political editorializing rule*, were adopted in 1967. The first requires stations to inform individuals or groups of attacks on their "honesty, character, integrity or like personal qualities" that occur during the discussion of controversial public issues. Those attacked must be provided with a copy of the offending statement within one week of the attack and must be given an opportunity to reply. The second rule requires stations that give editorial endorsement to one candidate to inform opposing candidates within 24 hours. Those candidates must be given a copy of the endorsement as well as a chance to respond.

D. Objections to these 1967 rules led to the 1969 *Red Lion* case, a crucial and unanimous Supreme Court affirmation of the fairness doctrine's constitutionality (see second Box).

E. Under the fairness doctrine, licensees make their own decisions as to (1) whether a subject qualifies as an issue of public importance, (2) how much time should be devoted to replies and when the replies should be scheduled, and (3) who should speak for opposing viewpoints.

F. In practice, stations can totally avoid airing issues of public importance with little risk of FCC objection. Only once has the FCC charged a station with a fairness-doctrine violation for failing to bring up an issue of great local importance.

G. Most fairness-doctrine complaints come from people reacting to ideas already discussed, rather than those who want to initiate discussions of new issues. The vast majority of these complaints are dismissed by the FCC, either because complaints fail to cite a legally definable controversial issue or because they fail to show that the overall programming of accused stations denied reasonable opportunities for opposing sides to be argued.

H. Cigarettes are the only advertised product that has ever been subject to treatment under the fairness-doctrine. The FCC ruled in 1968 that the advertising of cigarettes created a fairness-doctrine obligation and required stations to provide time for antismoking commercials. The 1972 Congressional ban on broadcast advertising of cigarettes brought an end to the issue.

I. Editorial advertising is accepted by some broadcasters. The networks and their owned-and-operated stations will not sell time for issue advertising. A 1980 survey indicated that about 90 percent of all other stations would be willing to consider such advertising on a case-by-case basis.

J. By the 1980s, an increasing number of critics suggested that the fairness doctrine be abolished. They claim that establishment of many new delivery systems weakens the scarcity rationale. Journalists claim that the doctrine has a chilling effect on public-affairs programming because of the constant need to consider that those with opposing views may demand time. Supporters of the doctrine note that most Americans now get much of their news and information from television and insist that the fairness doctrine simply encourages that all sides be heard.

K. In 1985 a marketplace-oriented FCC urged Congress to consider amending the communications act to eliminate the doctrine. It also encouraged broadcasters to initiate a case where the constitutionality of the doctrine would be tested and the *Red Lion* decision might be reversed.

18.5 Fairness and News

A. While bona fide news programs (those regularly scheduled and under licensee control) are subject to fairness-doctrine requirements, government officials generally defer to journalists' editorial discretion. Bona fide news stories are also exempt from the personal attack rule.

B. The FCC relies on journalistic discretion, but considers complaints about deliberate slanting, distortion, or withholding of the news. Few such cases get very far.

C. Politically oriented groups often charge stations or networks with news bias. Typically, such charges come from political conservatives, who believe news media and news personnel are too liberal in outlook. CBS has been the target of such complaints more often than ABC, NBC, or CNN, in part because it has carried more documentary programs than the other networks.

18.6 Political Broadcasts

A. Section 315 of the communications act requires stations that give or sell time to one political candidate to grant equal opportunities to all other legally qualified candidates for that office.

B. Originally, licensees could avoid demands for equal time by refusing use of their facilities to any candidate. Since 1971, Secion 312 requires stations to grant or sell "reasonable" amounts of time to candidates for federal elective office or risk revocation of their broadcast license. Further, time sold during the weeks just before elections must be priced at the "lowest unit charge" even though candidates might not ordinarily qualify for such discounts.

C. In 1959 the FCC ruled in the *Lar Daly* case that even a news broadcast involving a candidate was political "use" of broadcasting and, therefore, subject to equal-time obligations. Congress quickly amended Section 315 to grant four exemptions. They are: appearance by a legally qualified candidate on (1) a bona fide newcast, (2) a bona fide news interview, (3) a bona fide news documentary (if appearance of the candidate is incidental to the subject in the documentary), and (4) on-the-spot coverage of bona fide news events.

D. The equal-time rule applies both to candidates for party nomination in a primary election and to nominees in a general election.

E. Both presidential news conferences and debates between presidential candidates qualify as bona fide news events. The FCC ruled in 1983 that television networks or other media organizations could sponsor, as well as cover, political debates and still retain the bona fide news exemption.

F. Candidates do not have the privilege of decreeing when their ads will run. Nor, under a 1984 FCC ruling, may they use obscenity in their campaign materials.

G. The same regulations that apply to broadcasting stations apply to cable systems, but only to those channels on which the cable operator originates programming.

18.7 Issues in Content Regulation

A. Media conglomerates can exercise greater influence in the marketplace of ideas than do their smaller competitors. This is the principal rationale for various FCC rulings that limit the size of such conglomerates. Still, there is no guarantee that smaller stations will behave more responsibly than large, group-owned stations or systems.

B. The FCC and the courts seem to be moving away from the notion of access as a fundamental human right. However, the 1984 cable act calls for public- and leased-access channels.

C. First Amendment absolutists reject the concept of one law for broadcasting and another for press and motion pictures. They argue for First Amendment *parity*—equal treatment of all media.

KEY TERMS

A. *Cases and decisions*

Select one of the following decisions or cases for each of the statements that follow: *FCC v. Pacifica*, *Herbert v. Lando*, *Lar Daly*, Mayflower decision, *Miller v. California*, *New York Times v. Sullivan*, *Red Lion*, *Tornillo*, *Westmoreland v. CBS.*

1. Newspapers have the right to print what they choose. ______________________________

2. "It is the right of the viewers and listeners, not the right of the broadcasters, which is paramount." ______________________________

3. "...prohibits a public official from recovering damages for a defamatory falsehood unless he can prove that the statement was made with "actual malice..."

   ____

4. Complainants in libel suits have the right to examine tape archives, correspondence files, and program outtakes to determine the state of mind of reporters and editors.

   ____

5. In this libel case the complainant charged that his reputation had been ruined by a documentary program although, after a lengthy court battle, he abruptly withdrew his suit.

   ____

6. Community standards must be used in determining what is and what is not obscene.

   ____

7. Certain material was judged indecent, although not obscene because of the time of day during which it was presented. ______________________________

8. Early FCC decision, reversed in 1949, that prohibited licensees from broadcasting editorial opinions ______________________________

9. FCC interpretation that even a bona fide news-related broadcast involving a candidate was a political "use" of broadcasting that triggered equal-time obligations

   ____

B. *Sections, doctrines, principles, and rules*

1. Section of the Communications Act of 1934 that prohibits the FCC from censoring individual programs ______________________

2. Section that requires broadcasters to give equal treatment to all legally qualified political candidates ______________________

3. Section that threatens broadcasters with license revocation if they fail to provide candidates for federal office with reasonable access or refuse to let them purchase reasonable amounts of time ______________________

4. Legal term that refers to censorship of material to prevent it from being broadcast or disseminated ______________________

5. Published words that subject an individual to public hatred, shame, and disgrace are classified as ______________________. When such words are spoken, they are classified as ______________________. Both terms fall under the broader category of ______________________.

6. An ordinary citizen need only prove the falseness of a statement and the negative effect of that statement on his reputation in order to collect damages. Those classified as either ______________________ or ______________________ must also prove that the statement was made with ______________________.

7. The violation of an individual's physical solitude or the disclosure of details of an individual's private life may result in a suit charging ______________________.

8. The FCC's ______________________ principle has established the widespread distribution of stations and continues to promote the production of programs by those stations.

9. A 1946 FCC report titled *Public Service Responsibilities of Broadcast Licensees* is often referred to as the ______________________.

10. The FCC procedures that obligate stations to deal with controversial issues of public importance and to give time to qualified spokespersons with opposing points of view are known as the ____________________.

11. When a licensee holds a broadcast channel in trust for the benefit of the general public, the licensee is said to be exercising a ____________________ responsibility.

12. If an individual's honesty or integrity is questioned, the FCC's ____________________ rule requires the station to notify that individual within seven days.

13. If a station gives editorial endorsement to a political candidate, the FCC's ____________________ rule requires the station to notify all opposing candidates within 24 hours.

C. *Ideas and concepts*

1. The purpose of the First Amendment is to encourage and protect the exchange of concepts and opinions, thereby creating a ____________________ in which the truth will ultimately prevail.

2. Although the First Amendment affords protection from ____________________ censorship, it does not prohibit ____________________ censorship that might result in the selection and editing of material.

3. The threat of future punishment is said to have a ____________________ on the willingness of journalists to transmit facts and ideas to the public.

4. Hard-core pornography is classified as ____________________ and is not protected under the First Amendment. Less objectionable material is sometimes classified as ____________________ under a nuisance law that recognizes that something acceptable in one setting may be illegal in another setting.

5. News should be presented fairly and without bias or distortion, but the FCC is willing to grant journalists a great deal of ____________________ since it believes that a government agency should not act as an arbiter of truth except in the most blatant of circumstances.

6. To exempt those broadcasts that contained ____________________ from equal-time challenges, Congress amended the communications act in 1959.

7. Although the term *equal time* is widely used, the actual wording in the communications act calls for ______________________ for all legally qualified candidates.

8. Although the FCC is moving away from acknowledging a formal ______________ to broadcast facilities by individuals and groups, the cable act does mention the establishment of separate cable channels to be set aside for this purpose.

9. The term *First Amendment* ______________________ has become a slogan for First Amendment absolutists who believe that all media should be treated equally.

D. *Other terms*

1. Term used to describe a radio format that invited women to call in and talk over the air about their sex lives ______________________

2. Advertisements that address a controversial issue and present a point of view ______________________

3. Controversial CBS documentary that enraged political conservatives, generated charges that material was edited out of context, and led to attempts by a House committee to subpoena film outtakes ______________________

4. When political candidates buy airtime, they cannot be charged more than the ______________________ even though they might not ordinarily qualify for such pricing.

5. Groups interested in certain issues rather than specific candidates create special problems for the FCC. These groups are known as ______________________.

SELF-TEST

Fill in the Blank

1. The fundamental rights of freedom of speech and freedom of the press are found in the ______________________ to the U.S. Constitution.

2. List any two categories of speech that are unprotected and subject to punishment.

_______________ and _______________

3. For many years _______________ were banned from all courtrooms. They are now permitted in some state courts but not in federal courts.

4. A formalized set of procedures established by the FCC that obligates licensees to present controversial issues of public importance and provide time for alternative points of view is known as the _______________.

5. These procedures were challenged in court but affirmed by the Supreme Court in the _______________ decision, one of the most important legal cases in American broadcasting history.

6. For a brief period of time, broadcasters were required to carry without charge a specified number of commercials that presented an alternative point of view to the many commercials then advertising _______________.

7. Which network has most often been the target of complaints from the political right?

____

8. What kinds of programs are exempt from the equal-time obligations of Section 315?

____

9. The 1976 and 1980 presidential candidate debates were sponsored by a nonpartisan group, the League of Women Voters. However, the 1984 debates were presented by

_______________.

10. First Amendment absolutists call for regulatory parity that would guarantee the same treatment for print and _______________ journalists.

True/False

T F 1. Neither the FCC nor network officials may impose censorship on programs that deal with controversial issues.

T F 2. The *Tornillo* decision guaranteed political candidates the right to reply to attacks against them printed in newspapers.

T F 3. It is much more difficult for a public official to win a libel suit than it would be for an ordinary citizen.

T F 4. In obscenity cases, the context of the questionable material is relevant in the determination of a legal decision.

T F 5. Cameras and microphones are permitted in some federal courts but are not permitted in any state courts.

T F 6. Proponents of programming rules and guidelines argue that marketplace regulation does not work well for groups such as children, the elderly, and ethnic minorities.

T F 7. Public broadcasters do not have the right to editorialize under existing policy.

T F 8. When a licensee offers time for opposing points of view, it is the licensee that determines who should speak and how much time should be allocated for this purpose.

T F 9. The fairness doctrine has never been applied to broadcast advertising.

T F 10. Most television stations are willing to consider editorial advertising on a case-by-case basis.

T F 11. The FCC has recommended that Congress ame .. the communications act to eliminate the fairness doctrine.

T F 12. Bona fide news programs are not subject to fairness-doctrine requirements.

T F 13. Interview and talk programs such as those conducted by Phil Donahue and Larry King are exempt from equal-time requests.

T F 14. All of the FCC regulations dealing with political broadcasting that apply to radio and television stations also apply to cable systems that originate programming.

T F 15. Evidence indicates that smaller, single-owner stations are more responsive to community needs than are larger stations owned by groups or conglomerates.

PROJECT

The 1969 *Red Lion* decision is one of the most important in all of broadcast regulation. Why? Find out more about this decision. The text of the decision can be found in ed. Frank J. Kahn, *Documents in American Broadcasting*, 4th ed., Englewood Cliffs, N.J.: Prentice-Hall, 1984. Circumstances surrounding the case are presented in Fred W. Friendly, *The Good Guys, the Bad Guys and the First Amendment: Free Speech vs. Fairness in Broadcasting*, New York: Random House, 1976.

EPILOGUE

Future of Electronic Media

EPILOGUE

Future of Electronic Media

CHAPTER 19

Future Prospects

CHAPTER FOCUS

This concluding chapter raises questions about the future direction of broadcasting and cable in the next five to ten years. This chapter summarizes alternative points of view relating to technology, mass appeal, economics, and regulation.

CAPSULE

Main points from each section of Chapter 19 are summarized below.

19.1 Views of the Future

A. Two opposing views are considered. One proposes a radical change in the way individuals receive and utilize information and predicts the end of traditional broadcasting. The other view argues that changes in traditional broadcasting patterns will occur but that they will not come as fast or go as far as enthusiasts predict.

B. The radical view envisions a future where passive viewers will be replaced by active subscribers using home and office communications centers equipped with two-way channels for sending as well as receiving.

C. The conservative view suggests that consumers are not willing to provide the economic support necessary for radical change. The newer technologies do not provide fundamentally different services from those already available. They simply provide variations in combinations of services and in means of delivery—often at a significant increase in cost.

19.2 The Technological Future

A. Broadcasting still retains its unique advantage of "wirelessness." Cable and optical fiber may offer an interference-free environment, a greater number of channels, and two-way communication, but each delivery point is fixed and the physical link between delivery points is expensive.

B. The growth of backyard satellite reception by home users will slow, in part, because more satellite signals will be scrambled to prevent unauthorized viewing. Satellite reception by cable systems and broadcast stations will continue to expand because this method of transmission gives systems and stations flexibility in selecting program content.

C. High-definition television (HDTV) will be used initially in theaters where its need for very wide channels and special receivers will not be a limiting factor. Regular broadcasting of HDTV will probably not be feasible before the end of the century.

19.3 The Future of Mass Appeal

A. Traditional broadcasting appeals to an undifferentiated national audience. Cable, with its many channels, has the potential to appeal to specialized audiences, but this potential has been only partially realized. Cable syndicators, such as HBO, program to large national audiences. The growth of advertising on cable channels encourages cable programmers—as with broadcasters before them—to attract the largest possible audiences. Even VCR distributors concentrate on tapes with the broadest audience appeal.

B. Broadcast listenership and viewership is relatively stable and predictable. Cable subscribership is more volatile because cable introduces two new variables—the ability and the willingness to pay for the service.

C. Localized programming counters massification. Broadcasters usually have a stronger commitment to local program efforts than do cable operators. This is most evident in the area of news.

19.4 The Economic Future

A. Reduction of government regulation in favor of the marketplace has encouraged corporate mergers. The cost of developing media delivery systems and programming has become so great that smaller companies find it difficult to raise the capital necessary to survive.

B. The combined network share of the prime-time audience is expected to decline to about 80 percent. ABC, CBS, and NBC have diversified into other electronic media, especially cable programming services.

C. One selling point for pay cable is its lack of advertising clutter. Nevertheless, rumors persist that pay networks are considering a compromise whereby they will hold down increases in subscribers' rates but will add "tastefully inserted" advertising.

D. Public broadcasting's chronic need for funds, combined with advertiser desire to reach an upscale audience, will result in increasing use of advertising support in the 1980s.

19.5 The Regulatory Future

A. Broadcasting is the service most dependent on spectrum allocation as well as the service most readily available to the public. It is also still the most tightly regulated, despite considerable 1980s deregulation. Additional deregulation will generally be supported by the broadcasting industry but will be fought by many consumer groups and media competitors. Those who compare regulation to a pendulum believe that the pendulum will be stuck in the no-regulation position for years to come.

B. Critics of the fairness doctrine insist that the spectrum-scarcity argument no longer has relevance. They cite the fourfold increase in the number of radio stations since the doctrine was established. Supporters of the doctrine suggest that scarcity is still a factor and cite the multiple applicants for every broadcast channel as well as the ever-higher prices being paid for stations.

C. Critics believe the FCC's move to technological deregulation will delay innovation because both consumers and manufacturers are unwilling to invest in a technology that may become obsolete.

19.6 Conclusion

A. Radio and television have a combination of attributes that make them unique as media of public communication. Broadcasting's most important rival is cable television.

B. Future discussions must address whether broadcasting's continuing unique status should be preserved or whether the public-interest standard that has governed broadcasting for so many years should be replaced by economic controls of the marketplace.

KEY TERMS

1. This expanded form of stereophonic sound uses four channels rather than two but was rejected as unnecessary and costly by consumers. ____________________

2. This unique characteristic of radio and television gives broadcasting one distinct advantage over cable and fiber optics. ____________________

3. This term describes the tendency of broadcasting—and increasingly of cable as well—to place people into an undifferentiated national audience that ignores local and group differences.

____

SELF-TEST

True/False

T F 1. The elaborate home and office two-way communication centers that enthusiasts predict for the future require technical resources that are far beyond anything yet developed.

T F 2. The new technologies promise very different kinds of services from those provided by traditional radio and television.

T **F** 3. Backyard TV receive-only antennas can tune in satellite services and intercept unscrambled programs intended for delivery by broadcast stations or cable systems.

T **F** 4. Traditional broadcasting favors cultural conformity rather than cultural pluralism.

T **F** 5. Cable programming has become increasingly specialized as pay cable and advertiser-supported cable networks attempt to meet the interests of target groups within the general television-viewing audience.

T **F** 6. Competition from independent television stations and from basic and pay cable has reduced the network share during prime time from about 90 to less than 50 percent.

T **F** 7. The shift from landlines to satellites as the principal means of program distribution will encourage networks to increase the number of timely public-affairs programs they provide to station affiliates.

T **F** 8. Declining federal support will increase public broadcasting's dependence on advertising of one form or another.

T **F** 9. In the 1980s, FCC Chairman Mark Fowler has reversed the highly regulatory philosophy of his predecessor, Charles Ferris, and has redirected the commission toward new deregulatory policies.

T **F** 10. The FCC has refused to adopt technical standards for AM stereo, for teletext, and for DBS.

ANSWER KEY

CHAPTER 1

Key Terms

A. 1. British Broadcasting Corporation 2. Independent Broadcasting Authority 3. International Telecommunication Union 4. World Administrative Radio Conference 5. Radio-Tele-Luxembourg 6. United States Information Agency 7. United Nations Educational, Scientific, and Cultural Organization

B. 1. general Western European audience 2. Soviet citizens within the USSR 3. citizens of Eastern European Soviet bloc countries 4. Cuban citizens 5. anyone worldwide 6. Western European TV viewers 7. Eastern European TV viewers 8. anyone worldwide 9. anyone worldwide

C. 1. Soviet Union; direct government support 2. initially Britain and Japan; currently France, Sweden, other European countries; support comes from license fee revenue 3. initially and still to a large degree the United States; income is from advertising 4. currently Britain, Japan, U.S. (limited degree); combination of license fee revenue (taxes and contributions in U.S.) and income from advertising

D. The first measures only the number of people in the audience and is used in those systems that depend on advertising for support. The second measures the positive and negative values people assign to the programs they view and is used in those systems that utilize a license fee.

E. Pirate radio offers an alternative to establishment radio and generally emphasizes entertainment. Clandestine radio is operated by dissident political groups and offers a different, and frequently revolutionary, point of view.

F. Jamming is an intentional transmission designed to cause interference and prevent listeners from hearing certain radio signals. Transborder interference is unintentional but occurs when too many stations broadcast at or near the same frequency.

G. Communist bloc and Third World developing countries support the NWIO. Most developed countries oppose it.

H. Britain and Japan; British TV owners buy a license through the post office; in Japan collectors visit homes.

I. Cultural imperialism occurs when images, values, and concepts from another culture dominate media content. Western news values emphasize natural disasters, accidents, uprisings, and those "bad news" activities that deviate from routine daily events.

J. telephone, telegraph, satellite, computer data transfer, military communications, amateur radio, ship-to-ship and ship-to-shore communications, air traffic control information, weather data transmission, electronic navigational aids, police and fire dispatching, radio-controlled garage doors, cordless telephones, any other electronic transmission of voice or data.

Fill in the Blank

1. POBS (plain old broadcasting service) 2. interference 3. permissive 4. paternalistic 5. four, W, K 6. the BBC World Service 7. Canada 8. surrogate domestic 9. USSR and China

True/False

1. T 2. F 3. F 4. F 5. F 6. T 7. T 8. F 9. T 10. F 11. F

CHAPTER 2

Key Terms and Names

A. 1. Samuel F. B. Morse 2. Alexander Graham Bell 3. Thomas A. Edison 4. Lee de Forest

B. 1. James Clerk Maxwell 2. Heinrich Hertz 3. Guglielmo Marconi 4. David Sarnoff 5. Reginald Fessenden 6. Owen D. Young 7. Frank Conrad 8. William Paley 9. Herbert Hoover 10. Aimee Semple McPherson

C. 1. Reuters 2. Associated Press and United Press International 3. Agence France Presse 4. Tass 5. AT&T 6. Western Union 7. Western Electric 8. General Electric 9. Westinghouse 10. British Marconi 11. Radio Corporation of America (RCA) 12. 8XK 13. KDKA 14. DX 15. WJZ 16. WEAF 17. National Broadcasting Company (NBC) 18. NBC Blue 19. NBC Red 20. Columbia Broadcasting System (CBS) 21. Federal Radio Commission (FRC)

D. 1. vaudeville 2. kinetoscope 3. Morse code 4. transducer 5. patent 6. wireless 7. continuous wave 8. Alexanderson alternator 9. vacuum tube oscillator 10. the transistor and the silicon chip 11. attenuation 12. co-channel interference

E. The first involves the electronic (wireless) transmission of dots and dashes (Morse Code); the second involves the electronic transmission of voices, music, and a wide variety of sounds.

Fill in the Blank

1. mass media 2. Titanic 3. toll broadcasting 4. chain broadcasting 5. affiliates 6. Zenith Decision 7. Radio Act of 1927

True/False

1. F 2. T 3. T 4. T 5. T 6. F 7. T 8. F 9. F 10. T 11. T 12. F 13. T 14. F 15. T

CHAPTER 3

Key Terms and Names

A. 1. Paul Nipkow 2. Charles Jenkins 3. John Logie Baird 4. Philo Farnsworth 5. Vladimir Zworykin 6. Edwin Armstrong 7. Peter Goldmark

B. 1. William Benton 2. Lowell Thomas 3. Bing Crosby 4. Orson Welles 5. Norman Corwin and Arch Oboler 6. Edward R. Murrow 7. H. V. Kaltenborn 8. Sylvester "Pat" Weaver 9. Alan Freed 10. Charles Van Doren 11. John Henry Faulk

C. 1. "Dr." J. R. Brinkley 2. Reverend Charles Coughlin 3. James Caesar Petrillo 4. Elmer Davis 5. Allen B. DuMont 6. Senator Joseph McCarthy

D. 1. Mutual (MBS) 2. ASCAP 3. BMI 4. NAB 5. Press Radio Bureau 6. Office of War Information 7. ABC 8. WABC 9. Du Mont 10. Ampex 11. Desilu 12. AWARE

Fill in the Blank

1. fireside chats 2. Amos 'n' Andy 3. National Television System Committee (NTSC) 4. simulcast 5. Mercury Theater's "The War of The Worlds" 6. Chain Broadcasting Regulations 7. Sixth Report and Order 8. Top-40 programming 9. transistor 10. "McCarthyism"

True/False

1. F 2. T 3. T 4. F 5. T 6. T 7. T 8. T 9. T 10. T 11. F 12. T 13. T 14. F 15. T 16. F 17. F 18. F

CHAPTER 4

Key Terms

A. 1. community antenna television 2. television receive only (satellite antenna) 3. Home Box Office 4. subscription television 5. Multipoint Distribution Services 6. Multi-channel Multipoint Distribution Services 7. Instructional Television Fixed Service 8. Satellite Master Antenna Television 9. Corporation for Public Broadcasting 10. Public Broadcasting Service 11. National Public Radio 12. videocassette recorder 13. Direct Broadcast Satellite 14. high definition television

B. 1. booster 2. translater 3. parasitic 4. franchise 5. local origination 6. must carry 7. access channels 8. domestic satellite or Domsat 9. transponder 10. superstation 11. scrambling 12. videocassette recorder or VCR 13. video disc player 14. timeshifting 15. teletext 16. videotex 17. stereo TV

C. 1. Ted Turner 2. WTBS 3. Qube 4. U-matic 5. Betamax 6. VHS

Fill in the Blank

1. fragments 2. satellite 3. interactive 4. regulated 5. underwriting 6. rent

True/False

1. T 2. F 3. T 4. F 5. F 6. T 7. F 8. F 9. T 10. T 11. F 12. F 13. T 14. T 15. T

CHAPTER 5

Key Terms

A. 1. oscillation 2. frequency 3. attenuate 4. phases 5. velocity 6. wavelength 7. spectrum

B. 1. hertz 2. kilohertz 3. megahertz 4. gigahertz 5. microwaves 6. carrier wave 7. modulated 8. sidebands 9. bandwidth

C. 1. propagation 2. contours 3. direct waves 4. ground waves 5. sky waves 6. horizontal polarization 7. circular polarization 8. directional antenna 9. antenna gain 10. multiplexing 11. band compression

D. 1. pitch, loudness 2. overtones 3. analogue 4. digital 5. bit 6. allocation 7. subchannels

Fill in the Blank

1. electromagnetic 2. velocity (or speed) 3. 200 meters 4. digital 5. the highest available (atop a tall building or mountain) 6. effective radiated power (ERP)

True/False

1. T 2. F 3. F 4. T 5. T 6. T 7. F 8. F 9. F 10. T 11. F 12. F 13. T 14. T 15. F

CHAPTER 6

Key Terms

A. 1. co-channel interference 2. adjacent-channel interference 3. FCC assignment tables 4. clear, regional, local 5. Class II 6. Class I, Class III, and Class IV 7. Class D, Class A, Class B, and Class C 8. carrier current 9. Travelers Information Service (or TIS) 10. 107, 10 kHz 11. 100, 200 kHz (or .2 mHz) 12. 6 mHz, 600

B. 1. dynamic range 2. Subsidiary Communications Authorization (or SCA) 3. Voice of America 4. WRNO

C. 1. pixels 2. resolution 3. persistence of vision 4. flicker 5. target plate 6. scanning 7. deflection coils 8. frame, 30 fps, field, 60 fps 9. interlace 10. vertical resolution 11. blanking (or retrace) intervals 12. sync pulses 13. hue, luminance 14. compatibility 15. NTSC, PAL, SECAM 16. 525, 625 17. real time 18. sync generator 19. kinescope 20. transistors 21. time-base corrector 22. vertical blanking interval

Fill in the Blank

1. bandwidth 2. AM, FM, and TV 3. clear 4. 50,000 watts (or 50 KW) 5. Voice of America 6. motion, illumination 7. compatibility 8. electronic news gathering (or ENG)

True/False

1. T 2. T 3. T 4. F 5. F 6. T 7. T 8. F 9. T 10. F 11. T 12. T 13. F 14. T 15. F

CHAPTER 7

Key Terms

A. 1. syndication 2. network 3. relay 4. common carriers 5. coaxial 6. microwave relay 7. fiber optics 8. geosynchronous 9. prime meridian 10. C, Ku 11. uplink, downlink 12. transponder 13. footprint 14. low-noise amplifier (LNA), down-converter

B. 1. stylus 2. compact disc, laser 3. cassette 4. cartridge 5. kinescope recordings 6. quadruplex, transverse 7. slant, helical 8. U-matic 9. Betamax, VHS

C. 1. translaters 2. low power television (LPTV) 3. Instructional Television Fixed Service (ITFS) 4. Multipoint Distribution Service (MDS) 5. Multichannel Multipoint Distribution Service (MMDS) 6. teletext 7. direct broadcast satellites (DBS) 8. Community Antenna Television (CATV) 9. head-end 10. Community Antenna Relay Service (CARS) 11. trunk, feeder, drop 12. pay cable 13. interactive 14. Master Antenna Television (MATV) 15. videotex 16. cabletext

Fill in the Blank

1. delivery, distribution 2. phonograph records 3. magnetic tape recorders 4. video tape recorder 5. terrestrial 6. signal quality 7. the National Aeronautics and Space Administration (NASA) 8. Multipoint Distribution System (MDS) 9. very high, UHF 10. upstream

True/False

1. T 2. F 3. F 4. F 5. T 6. F 7. F 8. T 9. F 10. T 11. T 12. T 13. F 14. T 15. F

CHAPTER 8

Key Terms

A. 1. traffic 2. program log 3. make-good 4. availabilities 5. group owners 6. O & O 7. full-service 8. ad hoc 9. primary affiliates 10. secondary affiliate 11. independents 12. prime-time access rule 13. affiliation contract 14. network compensation 15. exclusivity 16. clearance 17. preempt

B. 1. Corporation for Public Broadcasting (CPB) 2. Public Broadcasting Service (PBS) 3. National Public Radio (NPR) 4. CPB-qualified 5. Station Program Cooperative

C. 1. churn 2. hard (or true), soft (or simulated) 3. Multiple System Operators (MSOs) 4. must carry 5. superstations

D. 1. Equal Employment Opportunities 2. American Federation of Television and Radio Artists (AFTRA) 3. Writers Guild of America (WGA) 4. Screen Actors Guild (SAG) 5. residual 6. IBEW, NABET, IATSE

Fill in the Blank

1. administrative, technical, programming, sales 2. O & O 3. network affiliates 4. every two years 5. the stations themselves (through the Station Program Cooperative) 6. subscriber fees 7. pay (or premium) 8. minorities, women 9. union 10. news and sales

True/False

1. T 2. T 3. T 4. T 5. F 6. F 7. T 8. F 9. F 10. F 11. T 12. F 13. F 14. T 15. T

CHAPTER 9

Key Terms

A. 1. local 2. network 3. national spot 4. cooperative (or local co-op) 5. sponsorship 6. participatory 7. scatter 8. zapping 9. clutter 10. split 30s 11. sponsor identification 12. billboards 13. spot announcement (or spot) 14. sustaining 15. station identification announcements 16. promotional announcements (or promos), public service announcements (or PSAs) 17. infomercials

B. 1. trafficking 2. upscale 3. cost per thousand (or CPM) 4. Standard Rate and Data 5. fixed, run-of-schedule (or ROS) 6. vertical, horizontal 7. preemptibility 8. rate grid 9. cable market of opportunity (or CMO) 10. trade deals (or trade-outs) 11. plugs 12. time brokers 13. per inquiry (or PI) 14. cold 15. Radio Advertising Bureau (or RAB), Television Bureau of Advertising (or TvB), Cabletelevision Advertising Bureau (or CAB) 16. national sales representatives (or national reps) 17. media mix 18. advertising agencies, billings

C. 1. program-length commercials 2. Continuity Acceptance, Broadcast Standards, Program Practices 3. Federal Trade Commission 4. Advertiser Substantiation 5. consent order 6. cease and desist 7. corrective advertising 8. Action for Children's Television (ACT) 9. host selling 10. plugola 11. payola 12. double billing 13. clipping

Fill in the Blank

1. sponsor 2. effectiveness 3. participating 4. station identification 5. audience measurement 6. audience size 7. commission 8. the stations that carried them 9. no regulation exists 10. children

True/False

1. T 2. F 3. T 4. T 5. T 6. F 7. T 8. T 9. F 10. F 11. F 12. T 13. T 14. F 15. T 16. T 17. F 18. F 19. F 20. F

CHAPTER 10

Key Terms

A. 1. economies of scale 2. syndicated 3. barter 4. deficit financing 5. above-the-line, below-the-line

B. 1. basic 2. tiers 3. pay-cable 4. addressable, pay-per-view 5. "scramble" 6. subsidiary communications authorization (SCA)

C. 1. trading up 2. trafficking 3. stand-alones 4. leveraged buy-out 5. Viacom

D. 1. underwriting 2. insulation 3. Temporary Commission on Alternative Financing for Public Telecommunications 4. enhanced underwriting 5. general support 6. *The Dial*

Fill in the Blank

1. videocassette recorders (VCRs) 2. news 3. 100 4. *TV Guide* 5. subscriber fees 6. Home Box Office (HBO) 7. SCA (or subcarrier) 8. AM stand-alones 9. 12, 25 percent 10. Capital Cities Communications, General Electric 11. Ted Turner 12. underwriting

True/False

1. T 2. T 3. T 4. F 5. T 6. F 7. T 8. F 9. F 10. F 11. F 12. T 13. F 14. F 15. T

CHAPTER 11

Key Terms

A. 1. parsimony 2. demographics, psychographics 3. conglomerates 4. window 5. stripping 6. electronic news gathering (ENG) 7. Independent Network News (INN) 8. UPITN 9. Operation Prime Time 10. Metromedia

B. 1. dayparts 2. prime time 3. fringe time 4. audience flow 5. flowthrough 6. outflow, inflow 7. counterprogramming 8. block programming 9. lead-in 10. stunting 11. bridging 12. vast wasteland

Fill in the Blank

1. women, 18–49 2. independent producers 3. theaters, pay cable 4. news and public affairs 5. summertime 6. morning and evening drive time 7. access time 8. blocking (or block programming)

True/False

1. F 2. F 3. T 4. T 5. F 6. F 7. T 8. F 9. F 10. T 11. F 12. F

CHAPTER 12

Key Terms

A. 1. genre 2. bimodal 3. upscale 4. clone 5. spin-off 6. situation comedies 7. action/adventure 8. made-for-television 9. made-for-pay 10. videos 11. sports anthology 12. commercial time-outs

B. 1. Nickelodeon 2. Action for Children's Television (ACT) 3. Children's Television Workshop 4. University of Mid-America 5. National University Consortium 6. public affairs 7. Cable-Satellite Public Affairs Network (C-SPAN) 8. *All Things Considered*

Fill in the Blank

1. little (or limited), great (or considerable) 2. 80 3. ABC 4. NBC 5. *Masterpiece Theater* 6. soap operas, game shows, talk shows 7. MTV 8. ESPN, ABC 9. on Saturday mornings 10. increasing 11. *60 Minutes* 12. seven

True/False

1. T 2. T 3. F 4. F 5. T 6. T 7. F 8. T 9. T 10. T 11. F 12. F 13. F 14. T 15. F

CHAPTER 13

Key Terms

A. 1. off-network 2. first-run 3. exclusivity 4. National Association of Television Program Executives (NATPE) 5. Prime-Time Access 6. access time 7. bicycling 8. barter 9. "happy talk" 10. "happy news" 11. news consultants 12. "action news" 13. "electronic church" 14. Oral Roberts 15. Jerry Falwell 16. M. G. "Pat" Robertson 17. Jim Bakker 18. Agency for Instructional Television (AIT) and Great Plains National Instructional Television Library (GPNITL)

B. 1. middle-of-the-road, older 2. country 3. automated 4. format syndicators 5. feature syndicators 6. adult contemporary 7. easy listening 8. information 9. all-news 10. Pacifica, "free-form"

Fill in the Blank

1. the evening newscast 2. three 3. satellites 4. public affairs 5. fundamentalist (or evangelical) 6. automated 7. rock 8. classical and jazz

True/False

1. F 2. T 3. T 4. F 5. F 6. F 7. F 8. T 9. T 10. T 11. T 12. F

CHAPTER 14

Key Terms

A. 1. Audit Bureau of Circulation 2. Arbitron 3. Nielsen 4. sweeps 5. Birch Radio 6. RADAR 7. diaries 8. meters 9. telephone coincidental 10. telephone recall 11. random digit dialing 12. people meters

B. 1. Area of Dominant Influence (ADI) 2. Designated Market Area (DMA) 3. elementary sampling unit 4. household 5. households using television, HUT 6. rating 7. share 8. cumulative, cume 9. reach 10. demographics

C. 1. sampling 2. random 3. sampling error 4. bias 5. response rate 6. stratified 7. weighting 8. penetration 9. least objectionable program (LOP) 10. tuning inertia

D. 1. penetration 2. timeshifting 3. Pay Cable 4. Electronic Media Rating Council (EMRC) 5. reliability, validity 6. hypoing 7. qualitative 8. focus groups 9. program analyzer 10 physiological 11 subliminal

Fill in the Blank

1. television and radio stations, advertising agencies 2. diaries, meters, telephone calls 3. the next day (overnight) 4. markets 5. household, individual 6. share, rating 7. seventy, seven 8. four

True/False

1. T 2. T 3. F 4. T 5. T 6. F 7. T 8. F 9. T 10. T 11. F 12. F 13. F 14. T 15. F

CHAPTER 15

Key Terms

A. 1. theory 2. process, models 3. effects 4. uses and gratifications 5. accommodation 6. subjective 7. sample surveys 8. content analysis 9. laboratory experiments 10. field studies 11. field experiments

B. 1. synthesizing of wants 2. loyalty 3. gatekeepers 4. agenda setting 5. prestige 6. staging 7. pseudoevents 8. news clips 9. publicity crimes 10. sunshine laws 11. Freedom of Information

C. 1. photo opportunities 2. "living room war" 3. sanitized 4. stereotypes 5. socialization 6. George Gerbner 7. desensitized 8. catharsis

Fill in the Blank

1. radio, motion pictures 2. television 3. models 4. content analysis 5. gatekeeping 6. Franklin D. Roosevelt 7. Eisenhower, Kennedy and Nixon 8. Vietnam, Grenada 9. prosocial, antisocial 10. televised violence

True/False

1. T 2. T 3. T 4. F 5. T 6. F 7. T 8. F 9. T 10. T 11. F 12. F 13. F 14. T 15. F 16. F 17. F 18. T 19. F 20. F

CHAPTER 16

Key Terms

A. 1. scarcity 2. commerce 3. titles 4 common carriers 5. broadcasting 6. public interest 7. spectrum use fee 8. National Telecommunications and Information Administration (NTIA) 9. Interdepartmental Radio Advisory Committee (IRAC)

B. 1. Copyright Act of 1976 2. public domain 3. retransmission rights 4. fair use 5. blanket licenses 6. Copyright Royalty Tribunal 7. signal piracy

C. 1. outtakes 2. *caveat emptor* 3. Federal Trade Commission (FTC) 4. Equal Employment Opportunities (EEO)

D. 1. boycott 2. Accuracy in Media (AIM) 3. WLBT, legal standing 4. public file 5. negotiated settlements 6. NAB codes 7. Radio and Television News Directors Association 8. National News Council

Fill in the Blank

1. commerce 2. president, Senate 3. Communications Act of 1934 4. common carriers, broadcasters 5. marketplace 6. copyright 7. cable systems 8. advertising 9. Congress 10. upheld 11. National Association of Broadcasters 12. more relaxed (or less rigid)

True/False

1. T 2. F 3. T 4. F 5. F 6. T 7. T 8. T 9. F 10. T 11. F 12. T 13. T 14. T 15. F 16. F 17. T 18. T

CHAPTER 17

Key Terms

A. 1. independent regulatory agencies 2. type acceptance 3. notice of inquiry, notice of proposed rule making 4. report and order 5. policy 6. ajudication 7. "raised eyebrow" 8. "jawboning" 9. family viewing time 10. advisory 11. ascertainment 12. program logs

B. 1. construction permit (CP) 2. mutually exclusive, comparative hearings 3. a franchise 4. nondelegable responsibility 5. public file 6. Federal Communications Bar Association (FCBA) 7. uncontested 8. petition to deny 9. administrative law judge

C. 1. National Cable Television Association 2. National League of Cities, National Council of Mayors 3. "PEG" 4. leased access 5. franchise fee 6. request for proposals (RFP)

D. 1. cross-media, 2. 12-12-12, 12 3. duopoly 4. grandfathering 5. tax certificates 6. distress sale 7. consent degree 8. due process 9. "show cause" 10. U.S. Court of Appeals for the District of Columbia Circuit 11. remand 12. writ of certiorari 13. revocation 14. short-term renewal 15. conditional renewal 16. forfeitures 17. ex parte 18. Mark Fowler

Fill in the Blank

1. five 2. civil service 3. Prime-Time Access 4. "must carry" 5. character, financial ability, technical ability 6. municipal (or local) 7. Equal Employment Opportunity (EEO) 8. postcard 9. actual past service or performance, proposed future service 10. ten, fifteen 11. twelve, twenty-five 12. licensee, FCC 13. short-term renewals, fines 14. lawyers

True/False

1. F 2. T 3. F 4. F 5. T 6. F 7. T 8. F 9. T 10. F 11. F 12. T 13. T 14. T 15. T

CHAPTER 18

Key Terms

A. 1. *Tornillo* decision 2. *Red Lion* decision 3. *New York Times v. Sullivan* 4. *Herbert v. Lando* 5. *Westmoreland v. CBS* 6. *Miller v. California* 7. *FCC v. Pacifica* 8. *Mayflower* decision 9. *Lar Daly* case

B. 1. Section 326 2. Section 315 3. Section 312 4. prior restraint 5. libel, slander, defamation 6. public officials, public figures, malice 7. invasion of privacy 8. localism 9. Blue Book 10. fairness doctrine 11. fiduciary 12. personal attack 13. political editorializing

C. 1. marketplace of ideas 2. state or government, private 3. chilling effect 4. obscene, indecent 5. editorial discretion 6. bona fide news 7. "equal opportunities" 8. access 9. parity

D. 1. "topless radio" 2. "advertorials" 3. "The Selling of the Pentagon" 4. "lowest unit rate" 5. political action committees (PACs)

Fill in the Blank

1. First Amendment 2. defamation, obscenity, plagiarism, invasion of privacy, inciting an insurrection 3. cameras and microphones 4. fairness doctrine 5. *Red Lion* 6. cigarettes 7. CBS 8. bona fide news 9. the television networks 10. broadcast

True/False

1. F 2. F 3. T 4. T 5. F 6. T 7. F 8. T 9. F 10. T 11. T 12. F 13. T 14. T 15. F

CHAPTER 19

Key Terms

1. quadraphonic sound 2. wirelessness 3. massification

True/False

1. F 2. F 3. T 4. T 5. F 6. F 7. F 8. T 9. F 10. T

To the Student

Please take time to tell us what you think of the *Study Guide* for *Broadcasting in America*, fifth edition. Your ideas can help us improve future editions of this book. Fill out the form and return it to College Marketing, Houghton Mifflin Company, One Beacon Street, Boston, MA 02108.

	Strongly agree	Mildly agree	Mildly disagree	Strongly disagree
1. The chapter focus and capsule sections were helpful summaries of the chapters.	☐	☐	☐	☐
2. The key terms sections were worthwhile exercises.	☐	☐	☐	☐
3. The short-answer or discussion questions were thought-provoking.	☐	☐	☐	☐
4. The self-tests helped me assess my understanding of the chapters and pointed out where I needed further study.	☐	☐	☐	☐
5. The projects were interesting to do.	☐	☐	☐	☐

6. What I liked best about this book is ______________________________

____

____

7. What I think should be changed in this book is ______________________

____

____